WINNING FOOTBALL DRILLS
FOR OFFENSIVE AND
DEFENSIVE LINEMEN

WINNING FOOTBALL DRILLS FOR OFFENSIVE AND DEFENSIVE LINEMEN

Bob Troppmann

Parker Publishing Company, Inc.
West Nyack, N.Y.

c. 2

© 1973 *by*
Parker Publishing Company, Inc.

West Nyack, N.Y.

Library of Congress Cataloging in Publication Data

Troppmann, Robert.
   Football drills for offensive and defensive linemen.

   1. Football coaching. I. Title.
GV954.4.T7   796.33'2077   72-5440
ISBN 0-13-960872-9

Printed in the United States of America

Dedication

To the Memory of Coach Joe Verducci

The Benefits for You in This Book

Each coach, during the off season, should chart all the activities that he thinks will make the up-coming season a winning one. This includes thinking through all the drills he has been using. The coach must ask himself if these drills have accomplished the job for him. For certainly drills have become an intricate part of football coaching and have become the number one topic of conversation at coaching clinics all over the country. Practice sessions are broken down into various drills, from individual techniques to drills that simulate game conditions.

Each drill must be designed so that both coaches and players know exactly what it is intended to accomplish. Whether it is going to be an agility drill, conditioning drill or whatever, the end result must be the improvement of some skill.

Most coaches have developed their own favorite drills and what may be good for one may not be good for another. The selection of drills becomes important in that it must teach a skill that will fit into the individual coaching philosophy. Hence, the coach must ask himself if the drill will fit into his system and just what does he expect from it. This book includes many line drills, some old, some new. The drills deal mainly with the internal linemen and are divided into the basic skills that the "men up front" must master in order to compete in today's game of football. Every drill has been tested in actual practice. Most of them have been used for many years.

Football today has become a game of reaction and movement and each drill must include these two basic ingredients. Movement is obviously the key to agility and quickness. The drill must also relate to a game-type situation because the player will be expected to do the same thing in a game that he does in a drill. There are some exceptions to this however, in that certain drills are designed to teach certain things, such as quickness or agility and it would look very odd indeed if three linemen suddenly did a "Monkey Roll" on the field during a game. Most drills are game orientated while others develop various skills and techniques. Drills also are designed so that players will react to certain situations through instinct and this only comes from a repetition of drills. We always relate the axiom that some skills eventually became natural skills such as when you "lift a fork, the mouth opens."

One simple technique is to have the best player lead each drill, this might change with various drills but it brings out the competitive spirit in the athlete who wants to be in the "front" of the line. Obviously the lead man will have to be changed from time to time to give other players who have shown improvement or who deserve a "shot at the top."

—Bob Troppmann

Acknowledgments

Appreciation is herewith expressed to those persons who have shared in the preparation of this book. The enclosed drills are an accumulation of twenty-five years in the coaching profession and it would be hard to single out any particular person for his originality. I am grateful to Mr. John L. Griffith, publisher of the *Athletic Journal,* and to Dr. Donald E. Fuoss, Athletic Director, Sacramento State College, for encouragement and permission to use materials from their publications. A word of thanks to all of the coaches that I have worked with and to Bob Muenter, Piedmont High School, for his constructive criticism.

To the late Coach Joe Verducci, who gave so much to this great game of football, I have dedicated this book. Finally, unending appreciation to my wife, Marilyn and the five J's—Jim, Joan, Jan, Judy and John —for their assistance, encouragement and unfailing support.

Contents

Dedication • v

The Benefits for You in This Book • vii

Acknowledgments • ix

Chapter One—Organizing and Coaching Winning Line Drills • 19

Formula for coaching linemen
Linemen are creatures of habit
Four basic types of line drills
Number of reactions for a good drill
Pattern or tempo for the drill
Competitive drills
Basic drills for a variety of drills
Drill time should be accounted for
Plan your time—time your plan
Coach must audit his program
Coach must develop his own philosophy
Exchange of ideas
Coach cannot become stagnant
No stationary position in football
Drills must get the job done
Good use of drill time
Master drill chart
Daily drill chart

Chapter One—Organizing and Coaching Winning Line Drills (cont.)

Sample of master chart
Sample of daily drill chart
Staff harmony and drill organization
Be conscious of stance and get off
Use a variety of drills
Hit or get hit
Run from a huddle
Master chart should be used
Drills should fit into your plans
Importance of running
Competitive drills
Setting up the drill
Coaches' enthusiasm
Over-doing a drill
Use the starting count and end with a whistle
Setting up the equipment
Marked areas for drills

Chapter Two—Winning Drills for Agility and Warm Up • 29

Major change in football organization
Time and place for each type of warm-up drill
Master plan
Calisthenics as a means of organization
Calisthenic formations by teams
Combining running with calisthenics
Pre-practice drills—early work
Sample of an early work chart

Drill 1 Indian Stripes	*To teach high knee action and balance*
Drill 2 Monkey Crawl	*To teach quickness, balance and quick recovery from the ground*
Drill 3 Quick Calls	*To work on reaction. Players react to a stimulus, either sound or movement*
Drill 4 Square Drill	*To warm up the team mentally. To be used in conjunction with the Quick Call drill*
Drill 5 Hurdle Steps	*To give a maximum all out effort for seven seconds*

Chapter Two—Winning Drills for Agility and Warm Up (cont.)

Drill 6 Dummy Crab   To develop quickness and agility while moving in a crab position

Drill 7 Barrel Run   To teach good balance and a maximum all out effort in seven seconds

Drill 8 Stretching   To stretch and loosen the hamstring muscles

Drill 9 Hurdlers Stretch   To lengthen the thigh and hamstring muscles and develop some flexibility in the hips

Drill 10 Carioca   To stretch and warm up, while developing good lateral movement

Drill 11 Scramble   To teach players to re-locate and to change direction

Drill 12 Modified Quarter Eagle   To help the stiff athlete, a player who has little movement from the hips

Drill 13 Prone Running   To teach players to recover from the ground while gaining momentum and to stress proper running form

Drill 14 Explosion   To develop explosion from a four-point stance

Drill 15 Monkey Roll   To develop quick movement and recovery off the ground and to work on proper method of recovering fumbles

Drill 16 Shuffle Seat Roll   To develop quick reaction to various keys and to work on proper techniques of shuffling, rolling and reacting from a football position

Drill 17 Supine Running   To teach players to recover quickly off their backs and to develop good running form

Drill 18 Relay Jack   To change the pace during the warm up period and to "jack them up" for the practice. Get them in proper frame of mind

Chapter Two—Winning Drills for Agility and Warm Up (cont.)

Drill 19 Wave Drill   *To teach and stress agility and reaction*

Drill 20 Mirror   *To teach quickness, agility and reaction*

Drill 21 Indiana Touch   *To teach quickness in lateral movement*

Drill 22 360 Degree   *To develop quickness of body movement and to locate the ball*

Chapter Three—Winning Drills for the Blocking Linemen • 57

The most important element in offensive football
The coach must decide his blocking needs
The coach should categorize his basic blocks
The coach should teach HOW to block before he teaches WHO to block
Proper stance and get off is a must
Blocking should be taught in a progressive manner

Drill 1 Shoulder Block   *To teach the proper fundamentals of the shoulder block*

Drill 2 Reverse Shoulder Block *To teach the reverse shoulder block*

Drill 3 Reverse Body Block   *To teach the reverse body block as a method of blocking to the inside*

Drill 4 Near Foot—Near Shoulder   *To teach the near foot—near shoulder block as one method of blocking a man to the inside*

Drill 5 Cross Body Block   *To teach the fundamentals of the cross-body block*

Drill 6 Reach and Scramble   *To teach an offensive lineman to cut-off a defensive man who is playing to his outside*

Drill 7 Step Jolt Drill   *To teach a blocker how to block an opponent when he cannot reach the defensive man on his initial charge*

Drill 8 Leverage Drill   *To teach blockers how to hit and use leverage after initial contact*

Chapter Three—Winning Drills for the Blocking Linemen (cont.)

Drill 9 Board Drill   *To develop balance, drive and toughness with the shoulder block*

Drill 10 Root Hog   *To teach a blocker to block under the hardest possible condition*

Drill 11 Indiana Circle   *To develop agility, balance and recovery from the four-point crab position*

Drill 12 Post Block   *To teach various methods of post blocking*

Drill 13 Lead Blocking   *To teach the lead block in conjunction with the double-team block*

Drill 14 Post and Lead   *To teach the post and lead or the double-team block*

Drill 15 Post—Lead and Slide   *To teach the post blocker to control the initial charge of the defensive linemen and slide to another opponent*

Drill 16 Shoulder Block vs Red Monster   *To teach how to hit, drive and maintain control and to stay with your man*

Drill 17 Combination Drill   *To work on all fundamental blocks using a two on two situation*

Drill 18 Six on Six   *To work on a combination of blocks*

Drill 19 Chute Drill   *To teach lineman to get off on the count and work on proper techniques of blocking*

Drill 20 King of the Cage   *To determine and encourage the "hitters"*

Drill 21 Around the Circle   *To teach blockers to block from a "football position" while moving*

Drill 22 Find the Backer   *To teach the offensive lineman to get off the line and find and make contact with the linebacker*

Chapter Three—Winning Drills for the Blocking Linemen (cont.)

Drill 23 Downfield Rec-   To teach and improve downfield
       ognition   blocking techniques

Drill 24 Burma Road   To develop balance, hitting position
and downfield blocking

Drill 25 Musical   To teach linemen to block downfield
       Dummies   and never to pass a potential tackler

Drill 26 Sled Progression   To teach your linemen the proper
way to hit the sled

Drill 27 Explosion Drill   To teach a blocker to bring his
upper body into play while blocking

Drill 28 Get-Off vs the   To stress good position and proper
       Sled   get-off

Drill 29 Hit and Recoil   To teach proper techniques in blocking and the ability to recoil and
block again

Drill 30 Form Block vs   To develop good form in blocking
       the Sled

Drill 31 React and Hunt   To develop balance and the ability
to react and move quickly

Drill 32 Across the Bow   To teach position, balance and
proper downfield blocking form

Drill 33 Piedmont Pad   To teach proper footwork and bal-
       Drill   ance while blocking for the passer

Drill 34 Push and Pull   To teach balance and footwork while
       Drill   blocking for the passer

Drill 35 Lovers Lane   To practice pass blocking

Drill 36 Drop Back Pass   To teach how to form a pocket
       Protection

Drill 37 Fundamentals of   To teach the fundamentals of pass
       Pass Blocking   blocking

Drill 38 Six on Six Drill   To teach pass blocking vs various
defenses

Chapter Three—Winning Drills for the Blocking Linemen (cont.)

Drill 39 *Progression Pass*   *To teach and review the basic pass*
        Protection Drill   *protection techniques*

Drill 40 *McQueary Blitz*   *To teach linemen to react to a line-*
        Blocking Drill   *backer over him*

Drill 41 *McQueary*   *To teach linemen correct timing in*
        Screen Pass Drill   *releasing for the screen*

Drill 42 *Blocking a Stunt-*   *To teach linemen to block against a*
        ing Defense   *stunting defense*

Chapter Four—Winning Drills for Pulling and Trapping Linemen • 107

Drill 1 *Correct Step*   *To teach linemen the correct steps*
       Drill   *in pulling*

Drill 2 *1–2–3 Trap*   *To teach the lineman the proper angle of approach*

Drill 3 *Trapping the Board*   *To develop correct techniques in the first steps of a trap block*

Drill 4 *Cal Drill*   *To check for speed, agility, balance and hitting*

Drill 5 *Funnel Drill*   *To check downfield blocking ability after pulling*

Drill 6 *Around the Hat*   *To develop speed and quickness in pulling*

Drill 7 *Cross Drill*   *To teach the linemen how to pull and fill for the quick trap*

Drill 8 *Guarding the Line*   *To find the best pulling lineman*

Drill 9 *5 on 5 Drill*   *To review all techniques of pulling and trapping*

Drill 10 *Pull and Seal Drill*   *To combine the seal block with sweep pulling*

Drill 11 *Quick Pitch Drill*   *To teach proper techniques of pulling for the quick pitch*

Drill 12 *3 on 3 Drill*   *To teach the guards the quick trap, to teach the guard to pull and lead*

Chapter Four—Winning Drills for Pulling and Trapping Linemen (cont.)

Drill 13 Sweep Drill — *To develop the correct pattern for running the sweep*

Drill 14 Trap vs the Stunts — *To work on the trap block vs stunts*

Drill 15 Pull and Cut Drill — *To check proper pulling techniques and to teach a pulling lineman how to pull and cut up field for a linebacker*

Drill 16 Trapping the Sled — *To stress good form in pulling out of the line, plus good hitting techniques*

Chapter Five—Winning Drills for the Defensive Line • 127

Drill 1 Stance Drill — *To work on the fundamentals of a good stance*

Drill 2 Step Drill — *To teach defensive lineman how to keep from over-extending*

Drill 3 Eagle Drill — *To teach reaction and to learn to fight pressure*

Drill 4 Forearm Lift — *To teach lineman how to use a forearm lift*

Drill 5 Forearm Shiver — *To teach and develop the forearm shiver*

Drill 6 Reaction Drill — *To teach down lineman to react to the various moves an offensive lineman will make*

Drill 7 Cluster Drill — *To teach the defensive linemen to get across the line and to avoid wrestling with the blocker*

Drill 8 Shooting the Gap — *To teach a defensive lineman to get across the line of scrimmage*

Drill 9 West Point Drill — *To teach defensive men to protect their area and react to the ball*

Drill 10 Splitting the Seam — *To practice breaking the double team block*

Chapter Five—Winning Drills for the Defensive Line (cont.)

Drill 11 Two on One — To teach the down defensive lineman to play and react to the pressure of the offensive blocker

Drill 12 5 on 2 Drill — To teach tackles to react to and play team blocking schemes

Drill 13 Across the Bow — To teach defensive linemen to shed a blocker and react to the ball carrier

Drill 14 Hit, Shed, Pursue and Tackle — To teach linemen to protect their area and to be ready to help in another area

Drill 15 Shed and Shuffle — To teach a lineman to step, hit and shuffle

Drill 16 Pursuit and Chase Drill — To teach a down lineman when to chase and when to pursue

Drill 17 Seat Roll vs Sled — To teach the seat roll vs the sled

Drill 18 Forearm Shiver on the Sled — To teach and practice the forearm shiver

Drill 19 Forearm Lift on the Sled — To teach and practice the forearm lift

Drill 20 Spin Out vs the Sled — To teach the spin out

Drill 21 Three on One — To develop the defensive man's reaction to a straight-on block, a fill block and a double team

Drill 22 One on One Fumble Recovery Drill — To practice recovering a fumble after disengaging a blocker

Drill 23 Hit and Pursue vs the Sled — To develop a good initial hit and proper pursuit of the ball carrier

Drill 24 Hit, Pivot and Pursue vs the Sled — To develop a good initial charge, control balance and good pursuit angle

Drill 25 Whirl Out Drill vs the Sled — Develop agility, balance, coordination and second effort

Chapter Five—Winning Drills for the Defensive Line (cont.)

Drill 26 Ten Twenty Drill   *To teach a defensive linemen how to strike a blow with the forearm shoulder lift and to be proficient with both left and right arms and shoulders*

Drill 27 Shed the Blocker   *To develop the ability to hit, come under control and hit again before pursuing*

Drill 28 Hit Pivot and Shed vs Sled   *To develop the ability to pivot out of a block and shed the second blocker before pursuing down the line*

Drill 29 Block Protection   *To teach and develop several methods of protecting the defensive man from the blocker*

Drill 30 Block Protection Rip and Lift

Drill 31 Block Protection Hand Shiver

Drill 32 Block Protection Slant Charge

Drill 33 Block Protection Loop Charge

Drill 34 Block Protection Dip Charge

Drill 35 Reaction Drill Sweeps or Pass   *To teach the down lineman the proper angles of pursuing or chasing and how to react to the pass*

Drill 36 Board Drill   *To teach a defensive lineman to neutralize, control and disengage his opponent*

Drill 37 Get to Them Drill   *To provide practice for the interior line in the pass rush*

Drill 38 Hit and Rush vs the Sled   *To teach how to neutralize the blocker, disengage and rush the passer*

Chapter Five—Winning Drills for the Defensive Line (cont.)

Drill 39	*Pass Rush vs the Sled*	*To strike a blow, read pass and rush the passer*
Drill 40	*Buckley Wall Drill*	*To teach defensive linemen to react to an intercepted or completed pass after they have rushed the passer*
Drill 41	*Mazzuca Speed Drill*	*To develop speed in getting off the hook to the passer*

Chapter Six—Winning Drills for the Tackling Linemen • 171

Drill 1	*Walk through Tackling*	*To teach the proper fundamentals*
Drill 2	*Confidence Tackling*	*To teach players how to tackle before they have live contact*
Drill 3	*Rhythm-Reaction and Tackle*	*To learn how to strike a blow and react to the ball carrier*
Drill 4	*Through a Man*	*To teach a down lineman to hit, neutralize, disengage a blocker and to tackle the ball carrier*
Drill 5	*Angle Tackling*	*To practice tackling from the side*
Drill 6	*Roll and Tackle*	*To teach proper form tackling and to develop increased agility by players reacting off the ground*
Drill 7	*Explosive Form Tackling*	*To teach players to explode through the numbers of a ball carrier from a hitting position*
Drill 8	*Sideline Tackling*	*To teach players to react to ball carrier's open field moves and to get in good position to make the tackle*
Drill 9	*Abe Martin Drill*	*To teach defensive ployers to react to pressure, get off the hook, and make the tackle*
Drill 10	*Triangle Drill*	*To practice tackling form and reaction*
Drill 11	*Through a Blocker*	*To teach a defensive man to shed a moving blocker and get to the ball carrier and make the tackle*

Chapter Six—Winning Drills for the Tackling Linemen (cont.)

Drill 12 Form Explosion   *To practice straight-on tackling*

Drill 13 Goal Line Tack-   *To teach the tackler to hit and drive*
*   ling*   *the ball carrier back instead of let-*
*   ting him fall over the goal line*

Drill 14 Oklahoma   *To teach linemen to react to a ball*
*   Tackling Drill*   *carrier after being knocked down*

Drill 15 Cat and Mouse   *To teach the tackler proper tackling*
*   form and how to stay with the ball*
*   carrier*

Drill 16 Obstacle Tack-   *To develop recovery, body control*
*   ling*   *and proper tackling form*

Drill 17 Tackling the Sled   *To stress good form and explosion*

Drill 18 Hit, Shuffle and   *To develp skill in adjusting quickly*
*   Tackle and Sled*   *from one alignment to another*

Drill 19 Form Tackling   *To develop proper form in tackling*
*   vs the Sled*
Drill 20 Seat Roll and   *To develop explosion while deliver-*
*   Tackle the Sled*   *ing a blow and quickness, agility and*
*   body control in locating the ball car-*
*   rier*

Drill 21 Hit and Hunt vs   *To teach how to deliver a blow and*
*   the Sled*   *react to the ball carrier*
Drill 22 Eye Opener   *To teach linebackers to read direc-*
*   tion. Help linebacker develop a nose*
*   for the ball*

Drill 23 Beatty Armless   *To teach position and leg drive for*
*   Tackling Drill*   *tacklers*
Drill 24 Square Tackling   *To develop tackling techniques with*
*   Drill*   *emphasis on intensity and balance*

Chapter Seven—Winning Drills for the Linebackers • 199

Best players on your team

Must possess agility, tackling ability, mental attitude and size

Called on to do many things, strong enough to neutralize blockers,
   diagnose plays, get to the ball and to cover on the pass

Drill 1 Keying Drill   *To teach the linebacker to react to*
*   movement*

Chapter Seven—Winning Drills for the Linebackers (cont.)

Drill 2 Half Bull — To teach linebackers to react to a block, regroup and be ready for the next blocker

Drill 3 Bull in the Ring — To teach backers to shed a blocker

Drill 4 Roll and Hit — To teach linebackers to ward off blockers

Drill 5 Mirror Drill — To teach linebackers to ward off blockers and keep their eye on the ball carrier

Drill 6 Scramble Drill — To teach linebackers to react to a ball carrier after using a defensive technique

Drill 7 Billy Goat Drill — To teach linebackers to ward off blockers, control his area and make the tackle

Drill 8 Scrape Drill — To teach linebackers to ward off blockers as they pursue to the outside

Drill 9 Mazzuca Bump — To teach linebackers to keep proper position on the ball carrier and to be in a good football position upon contact

Drill 10 Little Bull — To develop arm and leg action while delivering a blow

Drill 11 Tennessee Shadow Drill — To teach a linebacker how to keep a ball carrier from scoring

Drill 12 Linebacker One on One — To teach a linebacker to react to a blocker and to force a ball carrier

Drill 13 Shed and Tackle Drill — To teach linebackers to shed the blockers and to react to the ball

Drill 14 Dummy Dropper — To develop good balance while keeping the eyes open and the head up

Drill 15 Three on One Drill — To acquaint the backer with the blocking schemes

Chapter Seven—Winning Drills for the Linebackers (cont.)

Drill 16 Guard Reaction   To teach linebackers to read the
*   Drill   block of the offensive guard*

Drill 17 My Ball Drill   To teach linebackers to fight for the
*   ball*

Drill 18 Twenty Catch   To develop hand-eye coordination
*   Drill*

Drill 19 Tennessee   To teach a linebacker to get back in
*   Backer Drill   his zone and react to the QB*

Drill 20 Tip Drill   To teach a linebacker to catch a de-
*   flected ball*

Drill 21 Hand and Eye   To teach linebackers to react to the
*   Coordination   ball*

Drill 22 Through a Man   To teach a linebacker to play through
*   to the Ball   the receivers to the ball*

Drill 23 Bad Ball Drill   To teach a linebacker to react to a
*   poorly thrown pass*

Drill 24 Zone Coverage   To teach a linebacker to get in the
*   proper position in his zone*

Drill 25 Lateral Move-   To teach lateral movement in pass
*   ment Drill   defense*

Drill 26 Catching in a   To teach linebackers to intercept the
*   Crowd   ball in a congested area*

Drill 27 Fumble Drill   To teach linebackers to release a
*   blocker and react to a fumble*

Drill 28 Running the Line   To develop backward running and
*   change of direction*

Chapter Eight—Winning Drills for the Center • 231

Introduction—The center position, probably the most important posi-
    tion on the offensive line

Drill 1 Center Warm-Up Drills

Drill 2 Stance Warm-Up for the Center

Drill 3 Center's Stance

Chapter Eight—Winning Drills for the Center (cont.)

Drill 4 Center-Quarterback Exchange

Drill 5 Exchange Drill vs the Sled

Drill 6 Alternating Drill

Drill 7 Fundamentals of Blocking

Drill 8 Wrist Snap Drill

Drill 9 Centering for the Punt

Drill 10 Arm and Wrist Strength Drill

Drill 11 Speed and Snap Drill

Drill 12 Tire Drill

Drill 13 Leadership Drill

Chapter Nine—Winning Drills for in-Season Conditioning • 245

Drill 1 Rabbit Drill — *To develop speed and second effort*

Drill 2 Ups and Downs — *To develop quickness in getting off the ground and to develop second effort*

Drill 3 Giant Drill — *To develop high knee-action, balance and second effort during the conditioning period*

Drill 4 Homer Beatty Obstacle Course — *To develop balance, agility while working for conditioning*

Drill 5 High Stepper — *To develop high knee-action and good lateral movement while conditioning*

Drill 6 Northwestern Running Drill — *To teach second effort while developing conditioning*

Drill 7 Offside Desire — *To teach desire and second effort in downfield blocking while working on conditioning*

Drill 8 Whistle Drill — *To develop second effort*

Drill 9 Second Effort Drill — *To teach second effort in blocking and tackling*

Chapter Nine—Winning Drills for in-Season Conditioning (cont.)

Drill 10 Axt Drill	*To condition linemen while developing skills in the punting game*
Drill 11 Punt Coverage	*To condition linemen while teaching the skills of good punt coverage*
Drill 12 Punt Return	*To condition linemen while teaching the skills of a good punt return*
Drill 13 Kickoff Coverage	*To condition linemen while perfecting the kickoff coverage*
Drill 14 Kickoff Return	*To condition linemen while teaching the skills of a proper kickoff return*
Drill 15 Signal Drill for Running Execution	*To condition a team while working for proper execution in the running game*
Drill 16 Signal Drill for Passing Execution	*To condition linemen while working on the passing game*
Drill 17 Flash Ball	*To condition linemen physically and mentally*

Chapter Ten—Winning Drill for off-Season Conditioning Program • 267

Drill 1 Pre-Season Routine	*To build the body for the first days of football practice*
Drill 2 Flexibility Drill	*To develop body flexibility while getting ready for the season*
Drill 3 Cal Stoll Flexibility Drills	*To develop flexibility*
Drill 4 Quickness Builders	*To develop good habits of quickness and agility*
Drill 5 Wind Sprints	*To improve endurance and running form*
Drill 6 Combative Activities for Football Players	*To develop aggressiveness, initiative, proper footwork and control of the body*

Chapter Ten—Winning Drills for off-Season Conditioning (cont.)

Drill 7 Model Weight Program	*To administer a systematic off-season weight program*
Drill 8 Weight Training Program	*To improve physical conditioning through strength, speed, endurance power and agility*
Drill 9 Chuck Coker PTA Program	*High repetitions with heavy weights and minimum of rest*
Drill 10 Isometric Program	*To develop strength through static contraction*
Drill 11 Isotonic Exercise	*To build strength, develop endurance and increase flexibility*

Index · 291

WINNING FOOTBALL DRILLS
FOR OFFENSIVE AND
DEFENSIVE LINEMEN

CHAPTER ONE

Organizing and Coaching Winning Line Drills

Through the years a formula for coaching linemen has developed. The formula is simply:

$$\frac{\text{WORK} + \text{HUSTLE} + \text{MORALE}}{\text{KNOWLEDGE OF FUNDAMENTALS}} = \text{VICTORY}$$

It is the main objective of the line coach to teach the linemen the fundamentals of line play. This is done through hard work, repetition and proper direction by the coach. The end result is perfection and high team morale.

Linemen are a special breed and must be drilled and drilled hard to accomplish the skills needed to perform their tasks in football. There are basically four types of line drills. These are agility drills, reaction drills, conditioning drills and situation type drills. The coach must always have a purpose in mind when he chooses his drills in order to accomplish his objective. Football today is a game of movement and reaction and this should be remembered in selecting drills.

It is an old axiom that a drill must have more than one reaction to be classified as a good drill. A drill that lasts longer than six seconds and has more than four reactions becomes nothing more than a conditioning drill.

Another important point for the coach to be aware of is the pattern or the tempo that he sets for the drill period.

An attitude should be developed so that the linemen look forward to each practice session. Each day should be a "new day" as far as the squad is concerned.

Competitive drills make the best type of drills, but there are times when a drill should be made to be fun.

There may be a difference in philosophy in deciding whether certain basic drills should be used or a variety of drills should be used. The drill period for linemen is probably the toughest segment of the entire practice session and when players know that the same old drill for the same length of time will be used, they just go through the motions.

There are a hundred different ways to teach tackling, but by using several different tackling drills, team morale is built. On certain days, when a tackling drill is planned, the team may not be in the right mental frame of mind to go through it. However, the team needs work on this phase of the game. It is suggested that the coach look in his bag of tricks and come up with a tackling drill that has a little challenge or has a competitive angle to it. In other words, there are times when the coach must vary his drills.

Each minute of the drill period should be accounted for. The time for talking is before or after practice. To accomplish this, the coach should give each drill a name and go over it on the board with his players before he uses it on the field. Once the players know the objectives the drill and the name of the drill is called out, they will go through the drill without any questions and utilize the drill to the fullest.

PLAN YOUR TIME—TIME YOUR PLAN

Once the season has ended the coach should begin his off season program, attend all the clinics he possibly can and read all the technical books on football that he can get his hands on.

This is the time of year to "audit" the football program and to incorporate new ideas. The young coach must be careful however not to change his basic philosophy with every new thing he hears or reads or from what he sees on national TV every week. Each coach must develop his own philosophy and develop his own image. If a coach finds something he thinks will fit into his system he should use it but he should be sure that it ties in with his basic thinking. We are not all Duffy Daughertis or Bear Bryants. They may be doing something we would like to do or they may be people we would like to emulate, but the coach must remember his own liabilities and his strong points. He must coach by his own personality, must remember his success and must believe that what he is doing is right for him.

We are living in great times where the exchange of ideas has become a means to the end. The alert high school coach is as football oriented as the college coach because of the exposure that he has. Successful college coaches spend their winter months traveling around the country expounding on their theories of the game. To the high school coach it is like a smorgasbord dinner, he must pick and choose.

SUGGESTIONS FOR GOOD DRILL ORGANIZATION

Drills listed on a practice schedule do not always paint a true picture. If two or more drills are to be covered in a given period it is not uncommon for a coach to spend most of the time allotted on one drill and have the time run out just as he is getting into the next drill. By using the master chart the coach can check the actual number of minutes spent on each drill and if there is an unbalance, he can pick this up the next time he is working on that phase of the game.

MASTER DRILL CHART

The coach lists all of the drills that are to be covered in all categories, such as agility, blocking, pull and trap, pass-protection and so on. Each coach has his favorite drills and his own terminology for each segment of the game and will list each under the above categories. In addition, the coach will list the practice dates so that he will be able to chart the exact number of minutes spent on each drill, each day.

The master chart also acts as a guide to insure that all phases of the game are covered. As game time nears, the coach, by check-ing his chart, can be assured that everything has been covered.

The chart also tells a story upon the completion of a game especially if the players had a bad day in one particular skill such as tackling. By checking the chart the coach may find that very little time was spent on tackling. The master chart keeps the coach in tune with what he should be doing.

DAILY DRILL CHART FOR LINEMEN

Once the master chart has been devised it may also be used as a basis for making the daily practice plan. The drills are listed under the same categories as on the master chart.

During the staff meeting for example, the head coach will designate a block of time for a particular phase of the game and the line coach will just check the drills he desires and lists the amount of time he wants to spend on each one.

The daily drill chart also acts as a ready file for the coach and takes the guessing out of what he should do on a given day.

Once the practice session has been completed the line coach should go immediately to the master chart and list the actual time spent on each drill.

Paper work and the coach are not a very healthy combination especially in a school where there is a small staff. Once the charts are made however, there is very little paper work involved. It is just a matter of checking to see whether the job has been done properly.

It becomes a systematic way of organizing practice. Every item should be listed no matter how small.

Players should also be quizzed by the use of these charts to see that they have learned all that is expected of them. They will soon realize the purpose of each drill and what they are trying to accom-plish.

Actually the players are tested each game day, but to avoid "flunking" the final exam, they should be quizzed during the week. Coaches have a tendency to blame the players for mistakes, but perhaps the coaches should take the blame in some cases for not working long enough on a particular skill. It is not what the coaches know that makes a successful team, it is what they are able to teach that is important.

CHART 1 MASTER DRILL CHART FOR LINEMEN

The line coach will check the chart daily, listing the exact amount of time spent on each drill. All phases of the game should be added to this chart, only simple items are listed for the purpose of illustration.

Chart 1

Fill in minutes actually spent on each drill

DAY OF PRACTICE	1	2	3	4	5	6
AGILITY DRILLS	12					
Indiana Stripes	3					
Monkey Crawl	3					
Quick Calls	3					
Square Drill	3					
BLOCKING DRILLS	20					
Shoulder Block	5					
Leverage Block	5					
Board Drill	5					
Root Hog	5					
PULL AND TRAP DRILLS	15					
1-2-3 Drill	3					
Call Drill	5					
Cross Drill						
2 on 3 Drill	7					
PASS PROTECTION DRILLS	17					
Pad Drill	2					
Lovers Lane	10					
Six on Six						
Drop Back Drill	5					

CHART 2 DAILY DRILL CHART FOR LINEMEN

The coach fills in the number of minutes he desires to work on a certain drill. Only sample items are listed for the purpose of explanation of the chart. Each coach should list his own favorite drills in each category. This chart should be cross-checked with Chart 1 to see whether or not the time allotment has been equitable.

Chart 2

DATE _____ TIME _____ UNIFORM _____
PRACTICE NO. _____ DAY _____

Agility Drills	*Tackling Drills*
_____ Indiana Stripes	_____ Through a Man
_____ Monkey Crawl	_____ Roll and Tackle
_____ Quick Calls	_____ Form Explosion
_____ Dummy Crab	_____ Cat and Mouse
Blocking Drills	*Defense Line Drills*
_____ Shoulder Block	_____ Step Drill
_____ Leverage Drill	_____ Reaction Drill
_____ Board Drill	_____ Hit, Shed, Pursue
_____ Root Hog	_____ Seat Roll vs Sled
_____ Combination Drill	*Pass Rush Drills*
Pull and Trap Drills	_____ Speed Drill
_____ 1-2-3- Drill	_____ Pass Rush vs Sled
_____ Call Drill	_____ Wrestler Drill
_____ Cross Drill	*Linebacker Drills*
_____ 2 on 3 Drill	_____ Key Drill
Pass Protection Drills	_____ Half Bull
_____ Pad Drill	_____ Roll and Hit
_____ Lovers Lane Drill	_____ Mirror Drill
_____ Drop Back Drill	_____ Billy Goat Drill

HINTS FOR SUCCESSFUL DRILLS

Staff Harmony and Drill Organization

The Coaching staff must work in harmony so that the equipment will be available to all. For example, the whole team cannot work on the charging sled at the same time.

Always be Conscious of Stance and Get Off

Regardless of the drill, the coach must be conscious of the player's stance and that he gets off on the count. The drill is useless if linemen get sloppy.

Use a Variety of Drills

If you have a variety of drills so that you can do one drill one day and another drill the next, both of which are going to develop the same techniques, the players will learn a little faster. They will learn better because they will be a little fresher mentally and there is a little more imagination involved in doing something that is new. It is difficult to be enthusiastic doing something old.

Hit or Get Hit

Football is a game of contact and one is either doing the hitting or getting hit. A player who is not in a hitting position when he is within three yards of contact will not be the player doing the hitting.

Run From a Huddle

All drills should start from a huddle. The huddle should be five yards from the drill area. The coach calls the techniques to be used and the starting count and the players break and run to the line. This adds sharpness and organization to each drill, plus it is game orientated.

Name Your Drills

The coach will find that if each drill has a name it will be easier to set up the drill. Once the linemen understand the drill then the next time it is called the drill will be ready to go.

The Master Chart Should be Used

The coach should check the exact time spent on each drill and record it on the chart after practice. A drill may be set up for fifteen minute periods but in reality run only for seven minutes. The coach will note this on the chart and come back to the drill on another day.

Drills Should Fit into Your Plans

The drills should be designed to fit into your offensive or defensive plans. Each drill should be meaningful and have a definite purpose. Do not try to teach offense and defense at the same time.

Importance of Running

Since running is one of the basic fundamentals of football, players must learn to run well. Just to get out and run becomes a drudgery. Therefore, it is necessary to have a considerable amount of running in the drills and not have the players consciously realize they are doing it.

Competitive Drills

Football practice is tough by any standard, and if drills can become fun by being competitive, the execution of the drills should be better. Competitive drills make the best type of drills.

Setting Up the Drill

Never have more than three players in a line. Players cannot learn when they are standing around. They must be as active as possible.

Coach's Enthusiasm

The drill is only as good as the coach makes it. Enthusiasm is the key word. Explain the purpose of the drill to the players and remind them that each player must go all out in order to accomplish this purpose.

Over-Doing a Drill

Remember the purpose of the drill. If it is a technique drill, do not make it a conditioning drill. When a drill is over, do not take one more "hit." This defeats the purpose unless the drill is designed as such.

Use the Starting Count and End with a Whistle

Use the starting count or cadence that the team uses. Do this for each drill. Stop the drill on the whistle. This makes the drill game orientated.

Setting Up the Equipment

Equipment must be set up before practice so that valuable time is not wasted in moving it around. The ideal situation is to have certain areas designed for certain drills, with all the equipment in place and ready to use.

Marked Areas for Drills

Drills are best accomplished when the area is marked. Five-yard squares is one example of a marked area. Cones and markers should also be available. If line-marking is a problem, a fire hose can be substituted for a yard line. The advantage is that it can be moved from area to area depending on the condition of the turf. Another advantage is that the coach can paint the offensive numbering system on it to assure proper position in each drill. Marking the lines with diesel fuel is another aid in keeping the area properly marked. The lines are burned in and usually remain for the duration of the season.

Run Towards the Goal Line

In any team-function drill the team should always face the goal line. For example in running pass plays or signal drills the team should get in the idea of crossing the goal line. If the team is working on the twenty yard line and facing the other goal line it should run the full distance otherwise the players get into the habit of stopping in the middle of the field.

CHAPTER TWO

Winning Drills for Agility and Warm-Up

Probably one of the major changes in football organization is the warm-up period. Some coaches feel that mass calisthenics are the thing, some favor agility drills, some like the pre-practice weight program while others like isometrics or the exer-genie circuit. There are some coaches who use their pre-game warm-up as their daily warm-up plan, and then there is one school of thought that the players should warm-up on their own so valuable practice time is not wasted.

TIME AND PLACE FOR EACH TYPE OF WARM-UP DRILL

Our thinking is that there is a time and place for all types of warm-ups. On a given day, the mass calisthenics routine might fit the needs, this might be a time for team togetherness or team organization. Other days might be devoted to a group type warm-up drill in which each segment of the team does reaction and agility drills.

MASTER PLAN

By using a master plan the coach may vary his warm up drills and satisfy all of his needs. There is no one set way that works for all, teams vary and coaches vary. We have included various types of agility and warm-up drills that the coach may want to incorporate into his practice plan. Regardless of the plan however, coaches must be assigned and the warm-up period must be a meaningful period for all.

CALISTHENICS AS A MEANS OF ORGANIZATION

Before we leave this phase of the game we would like to suggest two types of formations that aid in practice organization. Probably the most popular calisthenic formation is where the entire squad lines up on the yard lines facing the coach. The squad lines up by teams, i.e. first team on the five-yard-line, second team on the ten-yard-line and so on. (See Diagram 2-1.) The staff uses this time to make any needed adjustments in team organization. As one coach leads the calisthenics the others move through the ranks and make the changes. By the time the exercise period is finished the teams are all in order and ready for the days practice. Scrimmage vests are used to designate the teams which further aids in drills as the team breaks for their group work. This bring up another point in drill organization. When several groups are used in a particular drill they should work by teams, the first team in one group the second team in another group and so on, this makes for more equal competition. It also aids in setting up the groups. For example, the coach will call the Greens in this group, the Golds in this group etc. If lines are formed for a particular drill then a member of the first team should lead each line, if the first team is wearing green vests for example, then there should be a "green man" heading each line. If the second stringer is doing a better job or showing more hustle in a drill then the "vests" should be changed on the spot.

If a squad is divided strictly by offense and defense the same organization can be used as described as above.

COMBINING RUNNING WITH CALISTHENICS

Another form of expediting the warm-up period is to have the teams form before they hit the field. The squad lines up by teams and the coaches make the necessary adjustments before they leave for the field. Once they hit the field they do what we call "stripes." The first team breaks off on the five-yard line, the second team

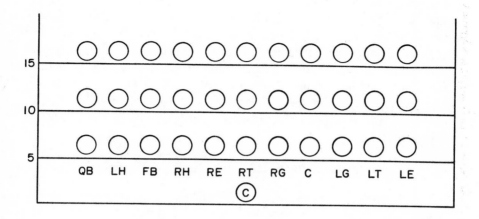

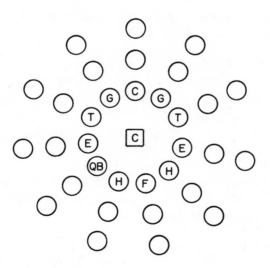

CALISTHENIC FORMATION BY TEAMS

Diagram 2-1.

CIRCLE

Diagram 2-2.

breaks off on the ten-yard line and the third team on the 15-yard line. They proceed back and forth across the field through the whole stripe procedure, this is listed under the agility drills and include high knee-action, cross stripes, carrioca, and run and balance. After a few days of explanation, this becomes automatic and it puts the team in the proper frame of mind as soon as they step on the field.

After they finish their stripes they line up for calisthenics as described above or for a change of pace may line up in a circle (see Diagram 2-2).

PRE-PRACTICE DRILLS—EARLY WORK

The early work period, usually a fifteen minute period before practice starts, should be used for special individual work as needed in certain areas or by certain players.

The coach will post a chart and have certain players and coaches report. This period should be well-planned and should not be used for a bull session. Players should never set one foot on a football field without having some objective in mind.

SAMPLE OF AN EARLY WORK CHART
(Posted in the locker room)

CENTERS—Coach Smith—Report 15 minutes early
        20 each, punt snaps and PAT snaps
        One block of each type (trap and wedge) on the charging sled
        Note: work on blocking to the left side
GUARDS—Coach Mazzuco—Report 15 minutes early
        Pulling to the left on the board
        Fifteen forearm and shoulder lifts on the two-man sled
TACKLES—Coach Mazzuco—Report 15 minutes early
        Pass protection vs the hanging dummy

The coach might just want to see a few players during the early work period or he may want to see his whole offensive line. This is a great chance for the coach to spend time with the players that are not receiving enough attention.

We believe that early work should not become a steady diet. It should only be used when a player or players are having trouble mastering certain fundamentals. The coach should make sure the players warm-up properly before beginning the early work.

TYPE OF DRILL: Warm-up—Agility
NAME OF DRILL: Indiana-stripes
TO BE USED BY: All Linemen
PURPOSE: To teach high knee-action and balance
SET UP:

1. Set up equal lines on the sideline opposite a yard stripe (Diagram 2-3).

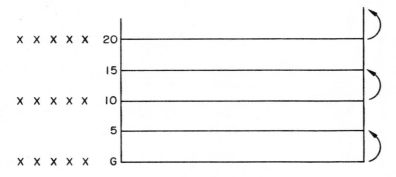

Diagram 2-3.

Instructions

1. The players line up facing the field.
2. On command from the coach, the groups proceed across the field moving in lock-step fashion keeping as close to each other as possible moving in unison with their same foot hitting the line at the same time.
3. Players will lift knees high and hit the yard line with their right foot.
4. When the groups reach the opposite sideline they will turn left to the next yard line and come back across the field, this time hitting the yard line with their left foot.
5. Once they reach the original sideline, they will start, this time using a cross-over step being careful not to touch the line.

Coaching points:

1. Players should use high knee-action with thighs parallel to the ground.
2. The coach should stress head up, eyes up and have players feel the lines. For proper frame of mind the players should keep in step.
3. This drill should be done at ¾ speed.

TYPE OF DRILL: Warm-up—Agility
NAME OF DRILL: Monkey-crawl
TO BE USED BY: All Linemen
PURPOSE: To teach quickness, balance and quick recovery from the ground
SET UP:

1. Set up 5 dummies, four dummies in a square and one dummy outside the square.
2. Make two set-ups so that the drill can be competitive (Diagram 2-4).

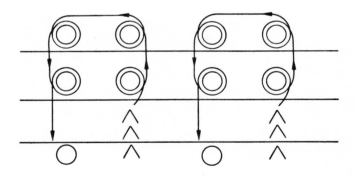

Diagram 2-4.

Instructions:

1. On command from the coach, players circle each dummy in a four point stance (crawl).

2. After circling all four dummies the player tackles the fifth dummy.

   Note: If the drill is used defensively, players tackle the fifth dummy. If the drill is used offensively, player shoulder block the fifth dummy.

Coaching points:

1. This drill should only be used about twice a week for a five minute period as it is a very tiring drill.

TYPE OF DRILL: Warm-up
NAME OF DRILL: Quick-Calls
TO BE USED BY: All Linemen
PURPOSE: To work on reaction. Players react to a stimulus, either sound or movement
SET UP:

1. Players line up by positions, facing the Coach or Captain (Diagram 2-5).

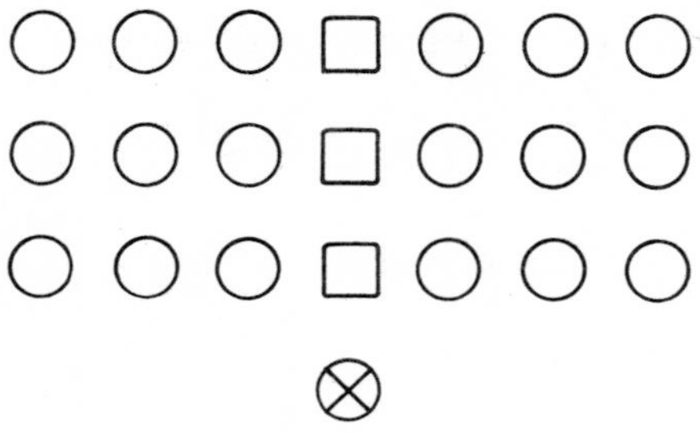

$$\bigcirc \; \bigcirc \; \bigcirc \; \square \; \bigcirc \; \bigcirc \; \bigcirc$$

$$\bigcirc \; \bigcirc \; \bigcirc \; \square \; \bigcirc \; \bigcirc \; \bigcirc$$

$$\bigcirc \; \bigcirc \; \bigcirc \; \square \; \bigcirc \; \bigcirc \; \bigcirc$$

$$\otimes$$

Diagram 2-5.

Instructions:

1. Players react to the movement of the leader.
2. If leader touches his helmet with his right hand the team reacts and "mirrors" the leader.
3. The leader goes through a ritual making certain moves and the team follows.

4. The team should be in a "football position," that is, bull neck, head up, back straight, legs flexed, good base.
5. This warm-up is designed more as a mental warm-up than a physical warm-up.

Coaching points:

1. This should be the first drill of the day. Once the team is sharp and the thinking muscles are ready then the coach should move to the next drill.
2. The coach or leader may use audios sounds, such as, hat, pads, knees. This gives the team a chance to react to sound as well as movement.

TYPE OF DRILL: Warm-Up—Agility
NAME OF DRILL: Square
TO BE USED BY: Offensive Linemen
PURPOSE: To warm the team up mentally. This drill may be used in conjunction with the Quick Call drill
SET UP:

1. Set up teams in a Square with the Coach in the center of the square (Diagram 2-6).

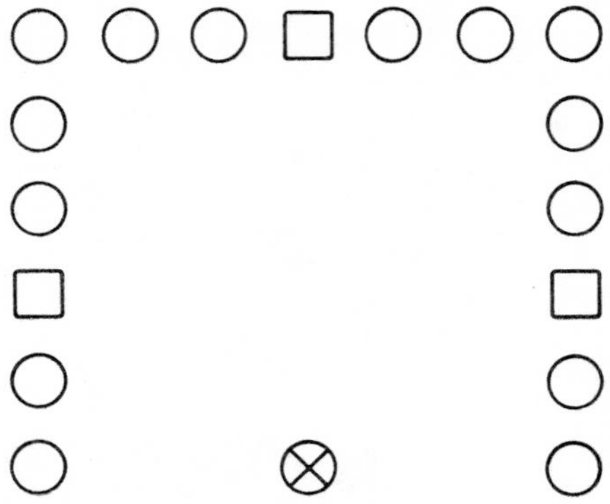

Diagram 2-6.

Instructions:

1. Players assume their offensive "ready" position.
2. Coach calls the play and the starting count and the linemen react by taking one step in the direction of their assignment.
3. The Coach may add to this drill by calling the type of defense that the team is facing.

Coaching points:

1. This drill can be used as a team drill, usually just before scrimmage to get the team mentally ready.
2. This drill is designed to discipline the team. It develops sharpness.
3. The drill also gives the Coach a chance to see if the players know their assignments.

TYPE OF DRILL: Agility
NAME OF DRILL: Hurdle-Steps
TO BE USED BY: All Linemen
PURPOSE: To give a maximum all out effort for seven seconds
SET UP:

1. A hurdle is placed in front of a player for him to hold while he runs in place (Diagram 2-7).
2. The coach uses a stop-watch to time the player for seven seconds.

Diagram 2-7.

Instructions:

1. On the starting signal, the player runs in place, bringing his knees up so that the thighs are parallel to the ground.
2. The player counts the number of times his right foot touches the ground in seven seconds.

Coaching points:

1. The same drill may be used with the player hopping in place while holding the hurdle.
2. On the starting signal the player hops, brings both feet off the ground trying to touch his thighs to his chest.
3. The player is timed for seven seconds and counts the number of times both feet hit the ground.
   (*Note:* Seven seconds is the estimated time of one football play)

TYPE OF DRILL: Agility
NAME OF DRILL: Dummy-Crab
TO BE USED BY: All Linemen
PURPOSE: To develop quickness and agility while moving in a crab position
SET UP:

1. Four dummies are placed in a circle area, two yards apart.
2. A player lines up on the top of one of the four dummies in a crab "all four" position (Diagram 2-8).

Instructions:

1. On the starting signal, the player moves left around the circle.
2. As the player moves around the circle he remains in a crab position with his hands facing the center of the circle. The player crabs over each dummy.
3. When the player has completed the circle he gets to a football position and moves laterally to a marker five yards away.
4. The coach uses a stop watch to time the player for seven seconds.

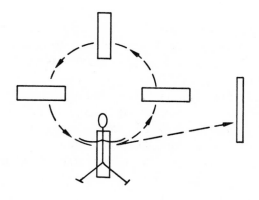

Diagram 2-8.

Coaching points:

1. The drill should progress until each player has moved left and right around the circle.

TYPE OF DRILL: Agility
NAME OF DRILL: Barrel-Run
TO BE USED BY: All Linemen
PURPOSE: To teach good balance and a maximum all-out effort for seven seconds
SET UP:

1. Place six dummies on their side, two yards apart.
2. Place the last dummy five yards away from the goal post or some such marker (Diagram 2-9).

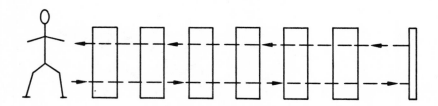

Diagram 2-9.

Instructions:

1. The player starts with his side facing the dummies.
2. The player uses a side running action or shuffle step across the top of the first dummy and progresses until he runs over all six.
3. Both feet must land inside each dummy.
4. After moving over the sixth dummy, the player touches the goal post (marker) and comes back over the dummies using the same running action.
5. Time is taken from the starting signal until the player has run for seven seconds.

Coaching points:

1. The coach should use a stop-watch and should check the players progress each day.
2. The same drill may be used with the players running straight ahead over each dummy.

TYPE OF DRILL: Agility
NAME OF DRILL: Stretching
TO BE USED BY: All Linemen
PURPOSE: To stretch and loosen the hamstring muscles
SET UP:

1. Players line up by positions, five yards apart (Diagram 2-10).

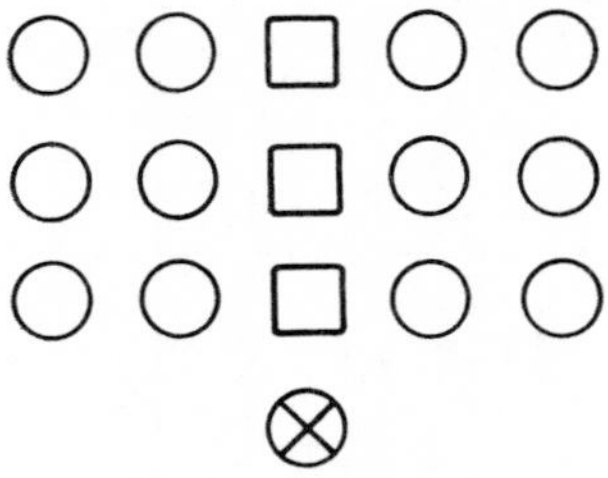

Diagram 2-10.

Instructions:

1. Players assume a football position and cross the left foot over the right foot.
2. On the starting signal, players bend down touching their thighs, knees, calves, feet and finally touching the ground on the count of ten.
3. At the count of ten they come to a standing position and cross their right foot over the left and repeat the exercise.

Coaching points:

1. This drill should be started slowly. That is, the players should not try to touch the ground until the count of ten.
2. Players should keep their head up as much as possible.

TYPE OF DRILL: Agility—Warm-up
NAME OF DRILL: Hurdlers-Stretch
TO BE USED BY: All Linemen
PURPOSE: To lengthen the thigh and hamstring muscles and develop some flexibility in the hips
SET UP:

1. Player line up by positions (Diagram 2-11).

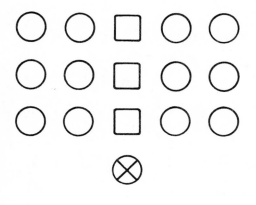

Diagram 2-11.   *Diagram 2-12.*

Instructions:

1. Players assume a sitting position on the ground.
2. Players extend the left leg forward pointing the toes upward.
3. The right leg is extended in such a way that the right knee is parallel to the right hip, the knee is bent at a 90 degree angle, the ankle is also bent at a 90-degree angle (Diagram 2-12).
4. On the starting signal, the players "bounce" and try to touch the right hand to the left foot while placing their helmet on their knee.
5. The exercise should take 10 counts and then the process should be reversed. The right leg extended and left leg bent at a 90 degree angle.

Coaching points:

1. This drill should be started slowly to avoid muscle pulls. The exercise should take 10 counts before the player touches his toes.

TYPE OF DRILL: Agility
NAME OF DRILL: Carrioca
TO BE USED BY: All Linemen
PURPOSE: To stretch and warm-up, while developing good lateral movement
SET UP:

1. Set up players on a yard line facing the coach.
2. The drill should progress the width of the field.

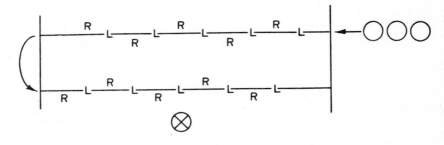

Diagram 2-13.

Instructions:

1. Players should be in a football position, head up, back arched, knees flexed and arms "hanging" in front of the body.
2. On the starting command, players move laterally across the field.
3. When moving left, the player steps laterally with his left foot, crosses his right foot in front of the left, steps laterally with his left foot, crosses the right foot behind and repeats this until he has crossed the field (Diagram 2-13).
4. Once the group reaches the sideline, the process is reversed. The player still faces in the same direction but now he moves right, back across the field. The steps are right laterally, left foot in front, right laterally, left foot behind, repeating the pattern until he has progressed the width of the field.

Coaching points:

1. The coach should "walk" the carrioca until the players have mastered the steps.
2. The players should try to develop a rhythmical rather than a mechanical move.

TYPE OF DRILL: Agility
NAME OF DRILL: Scramble
TO BE USED BY: All Linemen
PURPOSE: To teach players to "re-locate" and to change direction
SET UP:

1. Place four markers in a square, five yards apart.

Instructions:

1. The player starts with his right hand on the first marker.
2. On the starting signal, the player circles the first marker. He then proceeds to the second marker, placing his left hand on the marker and circles it to his left.

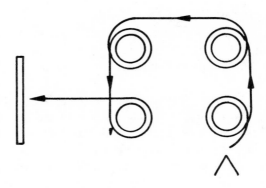

Diagram 2-14.

3. The player proceeds to all four markers, changing hands and direction at each marker (Diagram 2-14).
4. After the player has circled the fourth marker he sprints to the finish line which is five yards away.

Coaching points:

1. The players should be timed each time the drill is given to check his progress.

TYPE OF DRILL: Agility
NAME OF DRILL: Modified-quarter-eagle
TO BE USED BY: All Linemen
PURPOSE: To help the "stiff-athlete," a player who has little movement from the hips.

SET UP:

1. Players line up by positions, facing the coach (Diagram 2-15).

Instructions:

1. On the command of the coach, the players assume a football position and "chop" their feet.
2. The coach will say "right" and the players will jump and turn to the right with both feet hitting the ground.

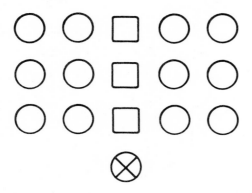

Diagram 2-15.

3. The player immediately turns back to the starting position.
4. The coach will say "left" and the process is reversed.
5. The important thing in this drill is that the shoulders and the upper body remains square facing the starting position, only the lower body moves in the direction given.

Coaching points:

1. It will take time to develop the proper body movement. At first the whole body will move in the direction called.
2. The ultimate however is just to have the lower body move. Hip flexibility is a must in the development of a football player.

TYPE OF DRILL: Agility
NAME OF DRILL: Prone-running
TO BE USED BY: All Linemen
PURPOSE: To teach players to recover from the ground while gaining momentum and to stress proper running form
SET UP:

1. Set up lines, three deep, one yard apart.
2. Front row in a prone position, hands in front, heads up (Diagram 2-16).

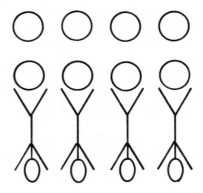

Diagram 2-16.

Instructions:

1. Coach moves foot, players drive forward clawing the ground with hands and feet gaining ground as they get to their feet.
2. Once players get to their feet they run 10 yards at ¾ speed stressing proper form, arms, hands, toes and legs driving ahead.

Coaching points:

1. Players must drive out, not up as they come off the ground.
2. Players should not stand up and then run.
3. Stress proper running form rather than speed after the players have come off the ground.

TYPE OF DRILL: Agility
NAME OF DRILL: Explosion
TO BE USED BY: All Linemen
PURPOSE: To develop explosion from a four point stance
SET UP:

1. Set up lines with three players in each line, one yard apart.
2. Coach stands facing the players (Diagram 2-17).

Diagram 2-17.

Instructions:

1. Front row of players assumes a good balanced four-point stance.
2. Coach moves backwards, players explode into a belly slam position, then regain a four-point stance.
3. Coach moves backward two or three times, each time players regain a four-point stance.
4. After two or three times, the coach shows sweep or pass and the players react.

Coaching points:

1. Players should explode out as far as possible.
2. Coach should stress the explosion plus getting back into a four-point stance.
3. Coach moves back to his original position and repeats the drill for the next people in line.

TYPE OF DRILL: Agility
NAME OF DRILL: Monkey-Roll
TO BE USED BY: All Linemen
PURPOSE: To develop quick movement and recovery off the ground and to work on proper method of recovering fumbles

SET UP:

1. Set up three lines, one yard apart, facing the coach.

Instructions:

1. Coach "pats" ball to start the drill.
2. Players are numbered, 1-2-3.
3. Player number two, the player in the middle, rolls to the right and resumes a four-point stance.
4. Player number one jumps over player number two and rolls over assuming a four-point stance.
5. Player number three jumps over player number one and assumes a four-point stance. (Diagram 2-18.)
6. Players continue this process until the coach is satisfied and then he drops the ball and calls "fumble." Players react to the ball and proceed to the end of the line.
7. The coach then starts with the next players in line.

Coaching points:

1. Players must keep their heads up in order to react to the fumble.
2. Stress proper roll and quick recovery.

TYPE OF DRILL: Agility
NAME OF DRILL: Shuffle-Seat-roll
TO BE USED BY: All Linemen
PURPOSE: To develop quick reaction to various keys and to work on proper techniques of shuffling, rolling and reacting from a football position

SET UP:

1. Set up two lines of players facing the coach. The players come up in a football position, feet shoulder width apart, toes pointed straight ahead, knees flexed, back arched, head up and bull neck, arms should be hanging in front of the body (Diagram 2-19).

Instructions:

1. Coach uses various signals for the players to react to either,

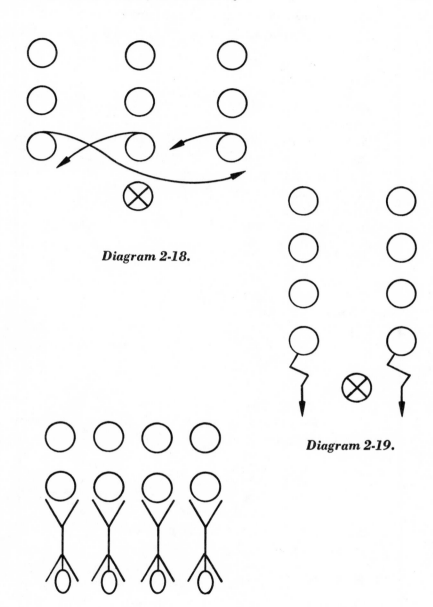

Diagram 2-18.

Diagram 2-19.

Diagram 2-20.

a shuffle, seat roll, or touching one knee to the ground.

2. After completion of the drill, players sprint 10 yards past the coach.

Coaching points:

1. When shuffling back and forth, players should remain in a football position.
2. When using a seat roll, players should drive the near knee down and in, and roll across his buttocks.
3. When touching knee to the ground the player should not use his hands to recover and should keep his head up and back arched.
4. After the players sprint 10 yards they resume their position at the end of the line.

TYPE OF DRILL: Agility
NAME OF DRILL: Supine-running
TO BE USED BY: All Linemen
PURPOSE: To teach players to recover quickly off of their backs and to develop good running form

SET UP:

1. Set up lines, three deep, one yard apart.
2. Front row reclines flat on their backs with their heads pointing toward the coach (Diagram 2-20).

Instructions:

1. On the command of the coach, the players roll over. (The coach will designate right or left.)
2. Players turn, recover from the ground and drive forward at ¾ speed.

Coaching points:

1. Players should turn over as quickly as possible.
2. Players should gain ground as they are getting up.
3. Coach should stress proper running form.
   Note: The coach has to sell this drill because players should

never be on their backs—but just in case it happens they should know how to react.

TYPE OF DRILL: Agility—Warm-up
NAME OF DRILL: Relay-jack
TO BE USED BY: All Linemen
PURPOSE: To change pace during the warm-up period and to "Jack them up" for practice
SET UP:

1. Set three dummies on their side, five yards apart.
2. Set three dummies in a "triangle' at the end of the three dummies.
3. Set up as many groups as possible, preferably by positions to have competition between the groups.
4. Set up equal line of players.

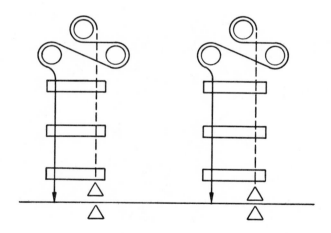

Diagram 2-21.

Instructions:

1. On the starting signal from the coach, the first player in each line will hurdle the dummies on the ground, do a figure eight around the triangle and hurdle the dummies on the ground and return to the end of the line (Diagram 2-21).

Coaching points:

1. The drill is finished when all players have completed the circuit.
2. The coach should stress competition by either a race against the stop-watch or against each group.
3. The coach should make sure that all players are properly warmed-up before they do this drill.

TYPE OF DRILL: Agility
NAME OF DRILL: Wave
TO BE USED BY: Defensive Linemen
PURPOSE: To teach and stress agility and reaction
SET UP:

1. Set up four lines with three players in each line.
2. Coach faces the players (Diagram 2-22).

Diagram 2-22.

Instructions:

1. The first row steps up, five yards away from the other players, in a four-point stance.
2. The coach may give audio signals or use a football to show movement.
3. The coach may use the following maneuvers:
   A. Forward, back, right, left.
   B. Forward roll, backward roll.

C. 360-degree right, player places right hand on ground and runs all the way around the hand. (Process reversed for 360-degree left.)

D. Lateral right or left. Players roll over and assume a four point stance.

E. Pass—players jump to block pass and come down to the ground with feet chopping.

F. Fumble—players dive out on their stomachs.

Coaching points:

1. When the coach finishes his maneuvers the players sprint 10 yards and get to the end of the line.

2. After the team knows the moves the coach will just be able to move the football for the maneuver he desires.

TYPE OF DRILL: Agility
NAME OF DRILL: Mirror
TO BE USED BY: All Linemen
PURPOSE: To teach quickness, agility and reaction
SET UP:

1. Set up two lines facing each other.

2. Designate one line as an offensive line and one line as a defensive line.

3. Place markers so that the offensive men and the defensive men are five yards apart (Diagram 2-23).

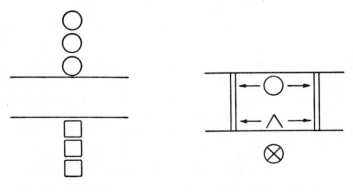

Diagram 2-23.   **Diagram 2-24.**

Instructions:

1. The offensive man makes any kind of move he so desires, that is he moves back and forth, does a forward roll, side roll or any move he can think of.
2. The defensive man copies or "mirrors" the offensive man and does the same thing that he does.
3. The idea of the drill is like "looking in a mirror."

Coaching points:

1. This drill should be used as a change of pace drill.
2. It has high morale qualities and enhances team spirit.
3. The more clever an offensive man can be the better the drill.

TYPE OF DRILL: Agility—Warm-up
NAME OF DRILL: Indiana-touch
TO BE USED BY: Offensive Linemen
PURPOSE: To teach quickness in lateral movement
SET UP:

1. Set up two men facing each other, five yards apart.
2. Place markers, five yards apart as the boundary.
3. Players line up in the middle of the five yard area, facing each other (Diagram 2-24).

Instructions:

1. The coach will give the starting command and the direction that both men will move, i.e. right or left. Both men will move in the same direction, that is they will "mirror" one another.
2. They will touch one marker, go back and touch the other marker and continue doing this for seven seconds.
3. This drill should be competitive and players should compete with players who are their own size.

Coaching points:

1. The coach will be able to find his quickest linemen with this drill.
2. Players may either turn and run to each marker or they may shuffle from side to side, whichever is the fastest for them.

3. Coach should stress the point that the shoulders should always be parallel to the line of scrimmage regardless of the method the player uses.

TYPE OF DRILL: Agility
NAME OF DRILL: 360-Degree-fumble
TO BE USED BY: All Linemen
PURPOSE: To develop quickness of body movement and to locate the ball
SET UP:

1. Set up four lines of players, three to a line, facing the coach.

Diagram 2-25.

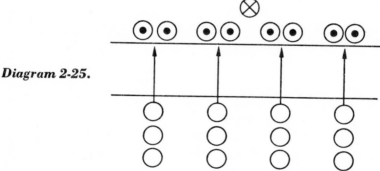

Instructions:

1. On the command from the coach, the first man in each line sprints five yards and explodes out and lands on his stomach.
2. The player then gets up and places his right hand on the ground and runs around his hand 360 degrees.
3. The player then places his left hand on the ground and runs around his hand 360 degrees (Diagram 2-25).
4. The coach yells "fumble" and the players locate and scramble for the ball.

Coaching points:

1. When the player is running around his hand, the coach should stress keeping his body as horizontal to the ground as possible with the head up.

CHAPTER THREE

Winning Drills for
The Blocking Linemen

"Blocking—the most important element in offensive football." The late Coach Vince Lombardi summed it up, "Football is two things, blocking and tackling. I don't care anything about fancy formations or new offenses or stunts on defense. If you block and tackle better than the team you're playing, you'll win."

The coach must first of all decide the type of blocking that is needed for his particular offense and categorize these blocks. Once the coach does a complete need-analysis of his blocking he will determine just what types of blocks his offensive linemen must master. For example, he may decide that his linemen must know how to use a left and right shoulder block, a left and right reverse shoulder block, a left and right near foot, near shoulder block, a crab block and a reach and scramble block. Once the needs are defined, the coach should select the proper drills for the teaching of these basic skills.

A common error among young coaches is that they teach WHO to block without teaching HOW to block; therefore blocking fundamentals should rate a high priority in the organizational plan.

57

A proper football position or stance is a must learn item before the techniques of blocking can be mastered. Unless an offensive lineman has a good stance and a good get-off he will never become a good blocker.

Blocking should be taught in a progressive manner, first against large dummies, or the charging sled, then to lighter dummies or arm shields and then finally live. A blocker must learn to HIT, LIFT AND DRIVE and must strive for perfection in these skills. The following pages have numerous drills, and the coach should pick and choose and perfect the drills that fit into his blocking scheme.

TYPE OF DRILL: Blocking
NAME OF DRILL: Shoulder-block
TO BE USED BY: Offensive Linemen
PURPOSE: To teach the proper fundamentals of the shoulder block
SET UP:

1. Players pair off, one man as a blocker and one man as the dummy holder.
2. Keep a maximum of three players in each line (Diagram 3-1).

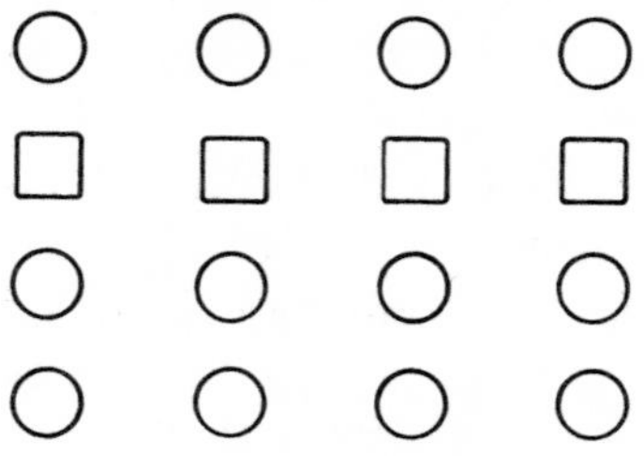

Diagram 3-1.

Instructions:

1. On the coach's signal, the blocker unloads into the dummy, with either the right or left shoulder, depending on the coach's call, and tries to drive the dummy back.

2. Concentration should be:
   A. Proper stance and get-off.
   B. Explosion into the dummy.
   C. Follow through.
   D. Moving the dummy.
      a. Coach stresses Hit, Lift and Drive.
3. The blocker should have his head up, bull neck, proper base, elbows extended, hand on his chest.

Coaching points:

1. Coach may want to start with just the hit and no follow through, then the hit and lift and finally the hit, lift and drive.
2. Coach should check the follow through.
3. Coach should also check the off arm. Some coaches desire the off arm to be held in at the chest, some use it as a lever on the ground.

TYPE OF DRILL: Blocking
NAME OF DRILL: Reverse-shoulder-block-to-a-crab
TO BE USED BY: Offensive Linemen
PURPOSE: To teach the reverse shoulder block as a method of filling to the inside
SET UP:

1. Players pair off, one man as the blocker and one man as the dummy holder.

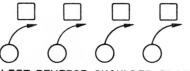

LEFT REVERSE SHOULDER BLOCK
LEFT REVERSE SHOULDER BLOCK

Diagram 3-2.

2. Blockers take one step to the right of the dummy for a right reverse shoulder block (Opposite for the left reverse block) (Diagram 3-2).

Instructions:

1. On the coach's command the blocker will pivot into the dummy hitting with the right shoulder. The blocker will drive the dummy laterally down the line of scrimmage.
2. After initial contact, the blocker will swing around into a crab position. The blocker is now facing the backfield. Using the principle of keeping the head between the ball carrier and the defensive man.

Coaching points:

1. The coach should be conscious of the blocker making contact first, before going into a crab position.
2. The process is reversed for the left reverse shoulder block.

TYPE OF DRILL: Blocking drill
NAME OF DRILL: Reverse-body-block
TO BE USED BY: Offensive Linemen
PURPOSE: To teach the reverse body block as a method of blocking to the inside
SET UP:

1. Players pair off, one man as a blocker and one man as a dummy holder.
2. Players take one step to the right for the right reverse body block and one step to the left for the left reverse shoulder block (Diagram 3-3).

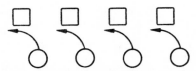

RIGHT REVERSE SHOULDER BLOCK
RIGHT REVERSE BODY BLOCK

Diagram 3-3.

Instructions:

1. The blocker pivots and whips his right arm across the front of the dummy.
2. At the same time the blocker whips his legs around to the rear of the dummy.
3. The blocker should now be facing exactly the opposite direction from which he started.
4. The blocker should now crab against the dummy, keeping his head between the ball carrier and the defensive man.
5. This is a stationary block rather than a moving block.

Coaching points:

1. The coach should make sure that contact is made on the initial move and that pressure is kept on the defensive man (dummy).

TYPE OF DRILL: Blocking
NAME OF DRILL: Near-foot-near-shoulder
TO BE USED BY: Offensive Linemen
PURPOSE: To teach the near foot-near shoulder block as one method of blocking a man to the inside

SET UP:

1. Players pair off, one man as the blocker and one man as the dummy holder.
2. Players take one step to the right for the left near foot-near shoulder and one step to the left for the right near foot-near shoulder (Diagram 3-4).

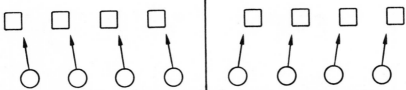

LEFT NEAR FOOT NEAR SHOULDER   RIGHT NEAR FOOT NEAR SHOULDER

Diagram 3-4.

Instructions:

1. The blocker steps toward the dummy with his foot closest to the dummy and hits with the shoulder closest to the dummy. That is, left foot, left shoulder to hit the dummy on the left and right foot, right shoulder to hit the dummy on the right.
2. The blocker must concentrate on quickness, it should resemble a jab in boxing. The blocker aims at the defensive man's hip.
3. The blocker must make contact on his first step.
4. The blocker must keep his head between the defensive man and the ball carrier.

Coaching points:

1. The blocker aims for a position where the defensive man will be after his charge, not where he lines up.
2. This block is usually used when a lineman pulls, and the outside man fills for him, or as a lead block in a double team block.

TYPE OF DRILL: Blocking
NAME OF DRILL: Cross-body-block
TO BE USED BY: Offensive Linemen
PURPOSE: To teach the fundamentals of the cross body block

SET UP:

1. Players pair off, one man as the blocker and one man as the dummy holder (Diagram 3-5).

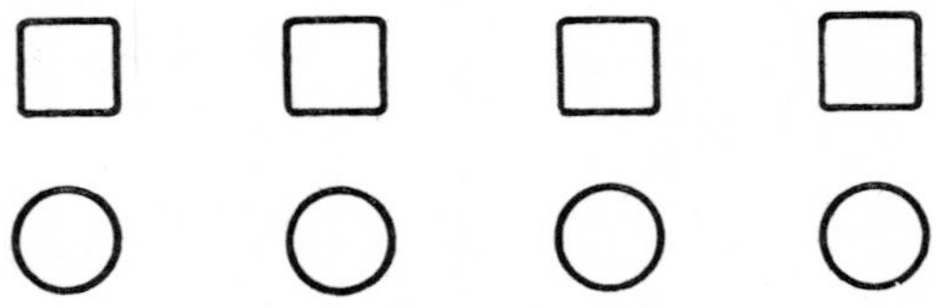

Diagram 3-5.

Instructions:

1. If the blocker is going to block with his right side he will:
   A. Shoot his right hand across the dummy about chest level.
   B. Contact the dummy with his right hip.
   C. Drive against the dummy, on all fours, using a crab like motion.
   D. The blocker should keep working so that his head is always between the ball carrier and the blocker.
2. Special emphasis should be placed on the speed of initial contact and the follow-up crab action.

Coaching points:

1. The coach should be conscious that the blocker does not leave his feet too soon or hesitate before making contact.
2. The object of the cross body block is to contact the defensive man and obstruct his path toward the ball carrier.

TYPE OF DRILL: Blocking
NAME OF DRILL: Reach-and-scramble
TO BE USED BY: Offensive Linemen
PURPOSE: To teach an offensive lineman to cut-off a defensive man who is playing to his outside

SET UP:

1. Players pair off, one man as the blocker and one man as the dummy holder.
2. The blocker takes one step to the left for the right reach and scramble and one step to the right for the left reach and scramble (Diagram 3-6).

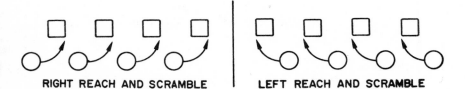

RIGHT REACH AND SCRAMBLE | LEFT REACH AND SCRAMBLE

Diagram 3-6.

Instructions:

1. On the command from the coach, the blocker crosses over with his inside leg and aims for the outside hip of the defensive man. When using a right reach and scramble, the blocker will step over with his left leg and make contact with his left shoulder. This will be just reversed for the left reach and scramble.
2. Once contact is made, the blocker scrambles around the defensive man using a crab motion. The head should be up and the blocker should be facing up field.
3. Once contact has been made with the shoulder, the blocker may go to all fours and crab the defensive man.

Coaching points:

1. Coach should stress contact with the shoulder before going to all fours.
2. Quickness in the first move should be emphasized due to the fact that the defensive man will be moving toward the ball carrier.

TYPE OF DRILL: Blocking
NAME OF DRILL: Step-jolt
TO BE USED BY: Offensive Linemen
PURPOSE: To teach blockers how to block an opponent when he can not reach the defensive man on his initial charge

SET UP:

1. Players pair off, one as a blocker and one as a dummy holder.
2. Dummies should be placed at three different intervals. One yard, two yards, three yards. Players will start with the one yard dummy then progress to the two and three yard dummies (Diagram 3-7).

Instructions:

1. All fundamental blocks may be used for this drill.
2. Players start with dummies one yard away, take a quick jab

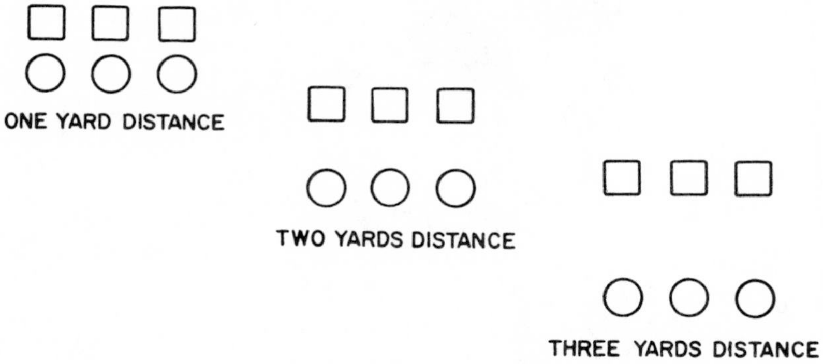

□ □ □

○ ○ ○

ONE YARD DISTANCE

□ □ □

○ ○ ○

TWO YARDS DISTANCE

□ □ □

○ ○ ○

THREE YARDS DISTANCE

Diagram 3-7.

step and then proceed with the various types of blocks.

3. The players finally block a "man" who is three yards away. This would simulate blocking a linebacker.

Coaching points:

1. The blocker must master the quick jolt step in getting to the defensive man, then he must use the proper techniques in blocking regardless of the type of block that is to be used.

TYPE OF DRILL: Blocking
NAME OF DRILL: Leverage
TO BE USED BY: Offensive Linemen
PURPOSE: To teach blockers how to hit and use leverage after initial contact

SET UP:

1. Set up five offensive blockers, guards, tackles and center vs a five man defensive line.

2. Use three different set ups (Diagram 3-8).
   A. Defensive men head up:

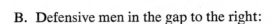

   B. Defensive men in the gap to the right:

   C. Defensive men in the gap to the left:

Diagram 3-8.

Instructions:

1. On the signal from the coach, the blockers will fire out and hit with the block as designated by the coach.
2. The coach should stress, get off, hit, lift and drive.

Coaching points:

1. This drill may be accomplished on the 7-man sled. However it is more functional against "moving" targets.
2. This drill should be done in rapid fashion, that is, get off, hit lift, drive, next group. The coach is looking for explosion and follow through on this drill.
3. This drill may be live or the defensive men may use dummies or arm shields.

TYPE OF DRILL: Blocking
NAME OF DRILL: Board
TO BE USED BY: Offensive Linemen
PURPOSE: To develop balance, drive and toughness with the shoulder block

SET UP:

1. Players pair off, one as a blocker and one man as a dummy holder.
2. The man holding the dummy will be stationed at the near end of a board (2 × 12 × 10 feet long) (Diagram 3-9).
3. Use as many set ups as feasible.

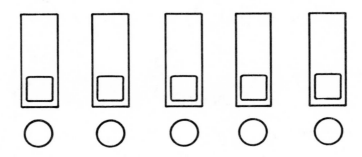

Diagram 3-9.

Instructions:

1. On the starting count, the offensive blocker will try to drive the dummy off the board.
2. If the drill is to be used live, the blocker will try to drive the defensive man off the board.
3. This drill may be used in a "chute" to keep the players "low."

Coaching points:

1. This drill can become highly competitive.
2. The "King of the Board Club" instills added incentive to this drill.

TYPE OF DRILL: Blocking
NAME OF DRILL: Root-hog
TO BE USED BY: Offensive Linemen
PURPOSE: To teach a blocker to block under the hardest possible conditions

SET UP:

1. Players pair off, one yard apart (Diagram 3-10).
2. Both players are on offense:

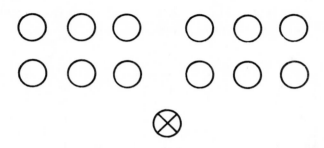

Diagram 3-10.

Instructions:

1. On the coach's signal, both men will charge and try to drive the other player back.
2. The emphasis should be on a fast LOW charge and good leg drive.
3. This drill can be enhanced if a rope is stretched across two dummies or the goal posts at a height of three feet. This insures the low charge.

Coaching points:

1. The coach will find that this drill builds up leg drive.
2. The coach will also find his most rugged players.
3. The coach will also find that the men that "win" these contests gain much respect from the rest of the team.

TYPE OF DRILL: Blocking
NAME OF DRILL: Indiana-circle
TO BE USED BY: Offensive Linemen
PURPOSE: To develop agility, balance and recovery from the four-point crab position
SET UP:

1. Set up a marker on a yard stripe.

2. Set up two standing dummies with holders on a yard stripe five yards away.
3. Set up two stations so that the drill may become competitive.

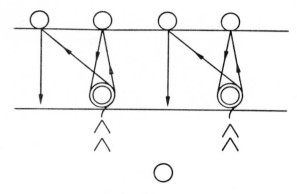

Diagram 3-11.

Instructions:

1. An offensive lineman lines up in front of the marker in a four-point stance.
2. On the signal from the coach, the players does a 360-degree spin around the marker, while in a crab position.
3. The player then crabs to the dummy on the right and shoulder blocks it, he returns to the marker, does a 360-degree spin around the marker and proceeds to the dummy on the left and blocks it (Diagram 3-11).
4. This is all done in a crab position.
5. The blocker holds the last dummy he hits, the dummy holder moves to the next dummy and that man gets in line.
6. The coach can have two groups going at once for competitive purposes.

Coaching points:

1. This is a grueling drill and should not be done for too long a period.
2. Players should "gather" before they hit the dummy. That is, they should get in a good hit position.

TYPE OF DRILL: Blocking
NAME OF DRILL: Post-block
TO BE USED BY: Offensive Linemen
PURPOSE: To teach various methods of post blocking
SET UP:

1. Players pair off, one man as a blocker and one man as a dummy holder (Diagram 3-12).
2. This drill is easier to use if the defensive lineman is "live." However if the drill is live it should be taught at 3.4 speed.

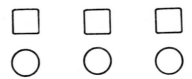

Diagram 3-12.

Instructions:

1. Three of the most common post blocks are:
   A. Blocker fires out and stops the defensive man charge by using a shoulder block.
   B. Blocker fires out and places his head under the crotch of the defensive man, lifting him off the ground.
   C. Blocker fires out and "removes" the inside leg of the defensive man.
2. Regardless of the type of maneuver used, the post blocker has as his main objective to set up the defensive man for the lead blocker.

Coaching points:

1. The emphasis is on setting up the defensive man.
2. The post blocker must neutralize the defensive man's charge.
3. Once the post block is mastered then lead blocker will work with him on the double team block.
4. The post blocker must step with his inside foot in order to close the seam between himself and the lead blocker.

TYPE OF DRILL: Blocking
NAME OF DRILL: Lead-blocking
TO BE USED BY: Offensive Linemen
PURPOSE: To teach the lead block in conjunction with the double team block

SET UP:

1. Players pair off, one man as a blocker and one man as a dummy holder (Diagram 3-13).
2. This drill is easier to teach if the defensive man is "live." However if the drill is live it should be taught at 3.4 speed.
3. The blocker sets up one yard to the right or left of the defensive man—depending on the call of the coach.

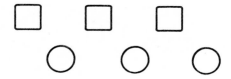

Diagram 3-13.

Instructions:

1. The lead blocker uses a near foot-near shoulder block.
2. The lead blocker should aim for the "arm pits" of the defensive man.
3. The lead blocker should assume that he is taking the defensive man by himself.
4. Once contact is made the blocker should drive the defensive man to the inside.

Coaching points:

1. The lead blocker must step with his inside foot in order to close the seam between the post man and himself.
2. Once the lead block is mastered, the post blocker will work with him to perfect the double team.

TYPE OF DRILL: Blocking

NAME OF DRILL: Post-and-lead
TO BE USED BY: Offensive Linemen
PURPOSE: To teach the post and lead or the double
                          team block
SET UP:

1. Set up groups of three players, two offensive linemen and one defensive lineman.
2. Place the defensive man head up (alternate right and left) (Diagram 3-14).
3. After the fundamentals have been mastered the defensive man may line up in any position he desires.

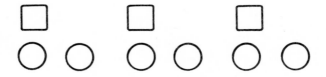

Diagram 3-14.

Instructions:

1. The post man has the main purpose of stopping the charge of the defensive man, setting him up for the lead block. He may:
   A. Drive head into mid-section, going to a shoulder block.
   B. Drive head under "crotch" and lift.
   C. Drive to the inside leg, taking the leg "away."
   D. Post man must step with his inside foot.
2. The lead man must figure that he has to take the defensive man by himself:
   A. Steps with his near foot and hits with his near shoulder.
   B. Aims above the hip of the defensive man.
   C. Uses head after contact to drive defensive man down the line.
   C. Keeps seam closed to the inside.

Coaching points:

1. Blockers' hips must be close together in order to close seam.

2. Lead man should drive defensive man to the inside and make a "pile."

TYPE OF DRILL: Blocking
NAME OF DRILL: Post-lead-and-slide
TO BE USED BY: Offensive Linemen
PURPOSE: To teach the POST blocker to control the initial charge of the defensive man and to slide to another opponent once the lead man makes contact

SET UP:

1. Set up players in groups of four.
2. Designate two players as the post and lead men and one man as the defensive man. One man shall be the linebacker (Diagram 3-15).
3. Set up as many groups as feasible.

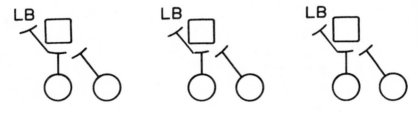

Diagram 3-15.

Instructions:

1. The down defensive man should be concerned with making an initial charge only. The linebacker will set in a regular linebacker position. The emphasis of this drill is on the offense.
2. The POST blocker will fire out (using one of the three types of post blocks), stop the initial charge of the defensive man and then SLIDE off and block the linebacker.
3. The lead blocker will end up taking the defensive man by himself.
4. The post blocker should NOT slide until the lead blocker has made contact.

Coaching points:

1. The defense should act as "dummies" until the skills are mastered.
2. The coach should make sure that the post man has an opportunity to slide both right and left.

TYPE OF DRILL: Offensive
NAME OF DRILL: Shoulder-block-vs-the-Red-Monster
TO BE USED BY: Offensive Linemen
PURPOSE: To teach how to hit, drive and maintain control and to stay with your man

SET UP:

1. A special type of sled is used. It is built out of a 2-man sled and the frame from an old car.
2. The sled is mounted on the front of the frame.
3. The coach sits in the "frame" and works the brakes and the steering wheel.
4. The foot brake stops the machine completely or lets it go with just enough pressure to make it roll (Diagram 3-16).
5. There are two hand brakes, one makes the machine turn left and one makes the machine turn right.

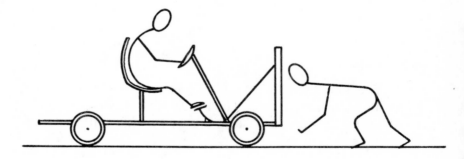

Diagram 3-16.

Instructions:

1. Two players line up in front of the pads and fire out with a shoulder block.

2. The coach will adjust the pressure and the direction. The coach lets the machine go to simulate a defensive man being driven back or applies pressure to simulate a defensive man neutralizing the charge.

3. The coach will also turn right and left in an effort to have the players stay with their blocks.

Coaching points:

1. The coach should be concerned with proper techniques:
   A. Proper stance and get off.
   B. Good hit position.
   C. Good leg drive, keeping leg, corresponding to the shoulder being used in front of the pad.

TYPE OF DRILL: Blocking
NAME OF DRILL: Combination
TO BE USED BY: Offensive Linemen
PURPOSE: To work on all fundamental blocks using a two on two situation
SET UP:

1. Set up groups of four, designate two players as offensive men and two players as defensive men.
2. Set up various combinations of defensive sets (Diagram 3-17).

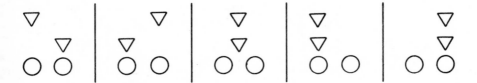

Diagram 3-17.

Instructions:

1. The offensive men will get in a huddle with the coach. The coach will call one of the following situations:

A. Left or right shoulder block   F. Double team
B. Reverse shoulder to a crab   G. Post and slide
C. Cross body   H. Trap and fill
D. Near foot-near shoulder   I. Wedge
                                     J. Pass protection

2. The defensive men will come across the line and protect their area and the offensive men will carry out their assignments.
3. The coach may set the defense any way he desires in order to work on certain fundamental blocks.
4. The coach can move from group to group and keep the drill moving at a fast pace while having a good look at all linemen.

Coaching points:

1. The drill may be live or be done with the defensive men holding dummies.

TYPE OF DRILL: Blocking
NAME OF DRILL: Six-on-six
TO BE USED BY: Offensive Linemen
PURPOSE: To work on a combination of blocks
SET UP:

1. The coach will set up six offensive linemen and six defensive linemen (Diagram 3-18).
   Note: The coach may use his basic formation. The above is set up for one tight end and one spread end formation.

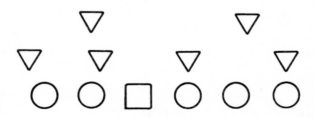

Diagram 3-18.

Instructions:

1. The offensive team gets in a huddle and the coach may either call certain fundamental blocks or call his team's rule blocking.
2. The coach can act as the quarterback and use the team's starting count.
3. This is also a good pass protection set up.
4. Once the basic moves are mastered the defense can line up in any position desired.
5. Once the season gets under way, the coach may want to set the defense in that of the up-coming opponent.

Coaching points:

1. This drill may be accomplished live or the defense may use dummies or arm shields.
2. This drill may be enhanced by using a full backfield on offense.

TYPE OF DRILL: Blocking
NAME OF DRILL: Chute-get-off
TO BE USED BY: Offensive Linemen
PURPOSE: To teach linemen to get off on the count and work on proper techniques of blocking
SET UP:

1. Set up six offensive blockers, a center and a quarterback in front of the chute.
2. Have six men holding dummies at the back of the chute (Diagram 3-19).

Instructions:

1. The six linemen line up in front of the chute.
2. On the starting count, given by the quarterback, the offensive linemen fire through the chute into the dummies.
3. The blockers will vary their blocks depending on the call of the coach.

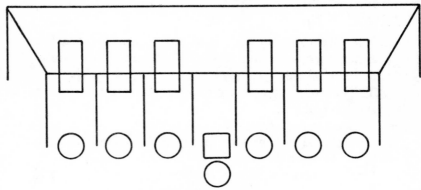

Diagram 3-19.

Coaching points:

1. Boards (2 × 12 × 8′) may be placed in front of the dummies to insure the wide base of the blockers' feet.
2. This drill may become live after the basic fundamentals have been mastered.

TYPE OF DRILL: Blocking
NAME OF DRILL: King-of-the-cage
TO BE USED BY: Offensive Linemen
PURPOSE: To determine and encourage the "hitters"
SET UP:

1. Place two offensive linemen head up in the cage (Diagram 3-20).

Diagram 3-20.

Instructions:

1. On the coach's signal each player tries to drive the other out of the cage using a shoulder block.
2. Stop the drill if either man's head hits the top of the cage.
3. Encourage low driving blocks.
4. Limit players to three turns per practice.
5. Stop the drill on the whistle.
6. Set up a challenge system.

Coaching points:

1. If cage is not available markers or dummies may be placed on the ground with the same results.
2. The "cage" becomes a good morale item however, if used properly.

TYPE OF DRILL: Blocking
NAME OF DRILL: Around-the-circle
TO BE USED BY: Offensive Linemen
PURPOSE: To teach blockers to block from a "football position" while moving
SET UP:

1. Place six men in a circle. Use as many circles as feasible.
2. The circle should have at least a five yard diameter.
3. The coach stands in the middle of the circle (Diagram 3-21).

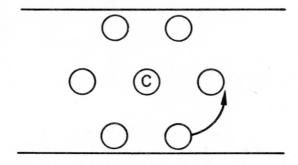

Diagram 3-21.

Instructions:

1. One man is designated as the blocker and proceeds around the circle using a shoulder block.
2. He takes only one hit at each man using either shoulder depending on his position as he moves around the circle.
3. The blocker should remain in a "football position" as he moves around, bull neck, back arched, legs flexed, good base, feet chopping.
4. As the blocker completes the circle, the next man proceeds around the circle in the same manner.
5. The men in the circle assume a football position and deliver a forearm lift as contact is made and return to their position in the circle.

Coaching points:

1. This drill may be live or the men in the circle may use a light dummy or arm pads.
2. This drill should be used sparingly.

TYPE OF DRILL: Blocking
NAME OF DRILL: Find-the-backer
TO BE USED BY: Offensive Linemen
PURPOSE: To teach the offensive linemen to get off the line and find and make contact with the linebacker

SET UP:

1. Place two men, with dummies, in the linebacker's position.
2. Place two men, with dummies on the line of scrimmage.
3. Place a blocker on the line of scrimmage between the two dummies.
4. The coach stands in front of the blocker.

Instructions:

1. On the coach's signal, the blocker will "fight" through the two dummies on the line of scrimmage. The men holding these dummies will keep pressure on the blocker but will let him through.

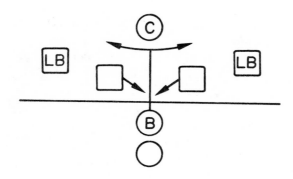

Diagram 3-22.

2. Once the blocker is about to break through the coach will point right or left and the blocker will block the linebacker (Diagram 3-22).

3. Players rotate so that they all get several chances to block.

Coaching points:

1. The blocker should keep his head up at all times, hence the coach points the direction for the blocker rather than using an audio sound.

2. Once the linebacker is found, the blocker should "run over him," shielding him from the play.

3. This drill may also be used live.

TYPE OF DRILL: Blocking
NAME OF DRILL: Downfield-recognition
TO BE USED BY: Offensive Linemen
PURPOSE: To teach and improve downfield blocking techniques
SET UP:

1. Set up six linemen on the line of scrimmage.

2. Place a marker one yard back and one yard outside the last offensive lineman.

3. Set up three standing dummies on each side in the "defensive backfield" to simulate defensive backs.

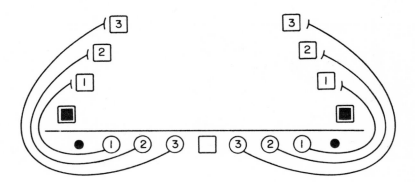

Diagram 3-23.

Instructions:

1. On the starting count the offensive linemen pull, around the marker and block down field.
2. The 1st man takes the 1st dummy, the second the next dummy and the third the last dummy (Diagram 3-23).
3. After the blocker hits the dummy he becomes the dummy holder and the dummy holder gets in line.
4. Players should alternate sides so that they pull left and right several times.

Coaching points:

1. The offensive linemen should gain depth as they pull, hence the marker on the line of scrimmage.
2. The blockers should gather and come under control before they block the "defensive man."

TYPE OF DRILL: Blocking
NAME OF DRILL: Burma-road
TO BE USED BY: Offensive Linemen
PURPOSE: To develop balance, hitting position and downfield blocking
SET UP:

1. Set up five dummies, with holders on the five yard lines.
2. Stagger dummies so that they are five yards apart.

DOUBLEHEADER

ROCHESTER RED WINGS

- vs -

GWINNETT BRAVES

Tue, Aug 10, 2010 6:05 PM

Frontier Field

Sec	Row	Seat	Price
219	G	1	$9.00

Incl.NYS Sales Tax & s.50 Monroe County Facility fee

CM   CASH
N BGW102
0

UPPER FULL

RED WINGS

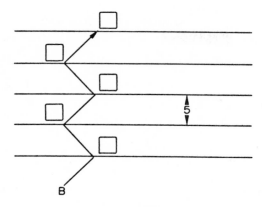

Diagram 3-24.

Instructions:

1. Players block the first dummy with the right shoulder, the second with the left shoulder and alternate until all five dummies have been blocked.
2. Upon hitting the last dummy, the blocker becomes the holder and all other holders move up to the next dummy. The player that was holding the first dummy gets into the blocking line (Diagram 3-24).

Coaching points:

1. The coach should stress proper football position when attacking the dummy. Head up, back arched, legs flexed, wide base and should explode through the dummy.
2. This is a good "hustle drill" and should be used at the end of practice.

TYPE OF DRILL: Blocking
NAME OF DRILL: Musical-dummies
TO BE USED BY: Offensive Linemen
PURPOSE: To teach linemen to block downfield and never to pass a potential tackler
SET UP:

1. Place six dummies with holders downfield.
2. Line up seven players on the line of scrimmage with their

backs to the defense. (Note: Do not let the offensive linemen see where the dummies are placed.)

3. The dummy holders may move the dummies anywhere they
   choose (Diagram 3-25).

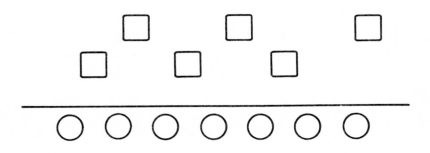

Diagram 3-25.

Instructions:

1. On the starting count the offensive men will turn, find a
   dummy and block it.
2. There will be one less dummy than there are offensive
   blockers so one blocker will not have a man to block and he
   will drop out of the drill.
3. This is an elimination drill. There should always be one less
   dummy than there are blockers. The drill proceeds until
   there are two blockers left and one defensive man.
4. After a man hits the dummy he becomes the dummy holder,
   the man that was holding the dummy gets in the offensive
   line.

Coaching points:

1. This drill should only be used on occasions. It is a high
   morale drill and should be used when practice gets sluggish.

TYPE OF DRILL: Blocking
NAME OF DRILL: Sled-progression
TO BE USED BY: Offensive Linemen

PURPOSE: To teach young linemen the proper way to hit the sled

SET UP:

1. Line up seven men in front of the sled (Diagram 3-26).

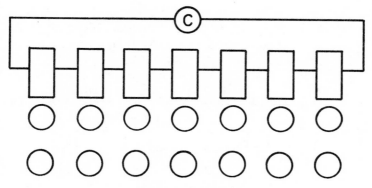

Diagram 3-26.

Instructions:

1. Start with hands on knees. Hit the pads with shoulder first then arm. The nose should brush past the pad, back should be arched. Then come back to a two point-stance.
2. Move players to a six-point stance (hands, knees, toes) and have them lunge out at the pads. Contact should be made with the shoulder pad first. After one "lunge" player gets back in line.
3. Move to a four point stance (hands and toes). Hit with shoulder first, drive sled a few yards.
4. Move to a three-point stance. Hit with shoulder first then drive sled a few yards.

Coaching points:

1. This is a good warm-up drill in early season before other basic sled maneuvers are used.
2. Coach should take time with this drill to insure the proper fundamentals on the sled.
3. Players should learn that they have to hit, lift and drive . . .

TYPE OF DRILL: Blocking
NAME OF DRILL: Explosion
TO BE USED BY: Offensive Linemen
PURPOSE: To teach a blocker to bring his upper body
                  into play while blocking

SET UP:

1. Line up seven men in front of the sled (Diagram 3-27).
2. Players assume a six point stance (hands, knees, toes).

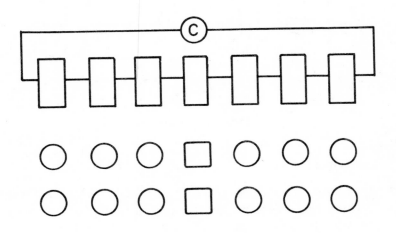

Diagram 3-27.

Instructions:

1. On the command from the coach, the players fire out into the sled.
2. Players should spring from their knees without using their feet.
3. After the first hit, they assume the six point stance, and hit the sled again.
4. The coach will call, hit, hit, hit, each time the players assumes his original stance.
5. This should be done three or four times in a row, then the next group of linemen come up to the sled.

Coaching points:

1. Coach should stress a stance that is coiled and ready for the hit.
2. Players should not "hitch" before they hit.
3. Player can roll right or left after the last hit and sprint ten yards downfield before getting back in line.

TYPE OF DRILL: Blocking
NAME OF DRILL: Offensive-get-off-vs-the-sled
TO BE USED BY: Offensive Linemen
PURPOSE: To stress good explosion and proper get off
SET UP:

1. Line up seven linemen on the sled.
2. A quarterback should be used for this drill. He will call the signals and take the ball from the center (Diagram 3-28).

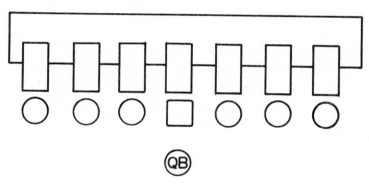

Diagram 3-28.

Instructions:

1. The quarterback and the linemen line up in a huddle five yards from the sled.
2. The quarterback will call the block and the starting count and break the huddle. Example of quarterback call: "Right shoulder block on 3. Ready, break!"
3. The linemen will explode into the sled and drive it two or three yards.

4. The quarterback will huddle the next line and the process is repeated.

Coaching points:

1. Backs may be added to this drill. They will line up at the end of the sled. On the starting count they will sprint 5 yards.
2. The quarterback should stress good huddle discipline, proper set at the line of scrimmage and proper get off.

TYPE OF DRILL: Blocking
NAME OF DRILL: Hit-and-recoil
TO BE USED BY: Offensive Linemen
PURPOSE: To teach proper techniques in blocking and the ability to recoil and block again
SET UP:

1. The seven-man sled or seven standing dummies may be used.
2. Players line up on the left of the sled/dummies and hit every other pad with their left shoulder.
3. Players then line up on the right of the sled/dummies and hit every other pad with their right shoulder (Diagram 3-29).

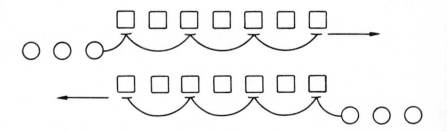

Diagram 3-29.

Instructions:

1. The first player in the line attacks the first pad and then hits every other pad.

2. The players must always be in proper hitting position before he hits the next pad.
3. The second man in the line follows the first man as soon as the first man hits the third pad.
4. Once all players have completed the circuit, then they start back with the other shoulder.

Coaching points:

1. The players may hit and come straight back or come out in a spin, locate and hit the next pad, depending on the wishes of the coach.
2. This drill teaches a player to be ready to hit, and to hit again.

TYPE OF DRILL: Blocking
NAME OF DRILL: Form-block-on-the-two-man-sled
TO BE USED BY: Offensive Linemen
PURPOSE: To develop good form in blocking
SET UP:

1. Set up two lines of blockers, one line in front of each pad.
2. Set up two men, with light dummies, one to the side of each pad.

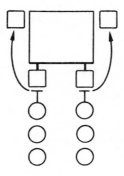

Diagram 3-30.

Instructions:

1. Players start from a knee position.
2. On the command from the coach, players deliver a blow to the sled with their shoulder.
3. They return to their knees and hit again (Diagram 3-30).
4. After three or four hits, they roll to the outside of the sled and use a form shoulder block on the man that is holding the dummy.
5. After they hit the dummy, they become the dummy holder, the dummy holder gets in the blocking line.

Coaching points:

1. Players should alternate lines so that they hit with the right and left shoulders. Player's head is always outside of the pads.
2. The progression of the drill would be from the knees, to a four-point to a three-point stance.
3. The main thing on this drill is the HIT, not the drive.

TYPE OF DRILL: Blocking
NAME OF DRILL: React-and-hunt
TO BE USED BY: Offensive Linemen
PURPOSE: To develop balance and the ability to react and move quickly
SET UP:

1. Set up four lines of players facing the coach.
2. Set up four men holding dummies five yards away and in front of each line.
3. Coach stands in the center of the blockers, two yards away.

Instructions:

1. Players assume a football position.
2. On the command by the coach, the players start chopping their feet.
3. The coach gives the directional signal, Right, Left. Players do a ½ turn in the designated direction when the coach says TURN.

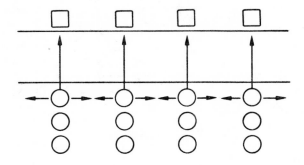

Diagram 3-31.

4. On the command HUNT, the players take off and fire into the dummy with a shoulder block (Diagram 3-31).
5. Coach may keep the commands going, i.e. Right, Left, Left, Right, Turn, Hunt.

Coaching points:

1. Emphasize quick feet, staying in a football position at all times.
2. Coach should keep each player moving for 10 or 15 seconds.

TYPE OF DRILL: Blocking
NAME OF DRILL: Across-the-bow
TO BE USED BY: Offensive Linemen
PURPOSE: To teach position, balance and proper down-field blocking form
SET UP:

1. Players pair off on a yard line.
2. Drill should progress the width of the field.
3. Designate one line as the blockers and one line as the defensive men.

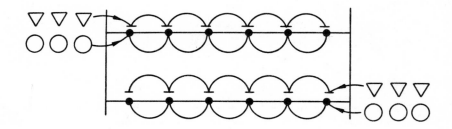

Diagram 3-32.

Instructions:

1. On the command of the coach the players will proceed across the field each staying on his side of the yard stripe.
2. The offensive player will attempt to get his head and shoulder in front of the defensive man. The blocker should aim for the far hip of the defensive man.
3. The defensive man will use a forearm shiver and try to keep the blocker off of him. The defensive man will just take one shot each time with his hands.
4. The offensive man will attempt to get his head and shoulders in front of the defensive man, when he is pushed off, he will recoil and try again.
5. When the players reach the other side of the field, the defensive man becomes the blocker and the blocker the defensive man (Diagram 3-32).

Coaching points:

1. Drill should be walked through to insure proper techniques.

TYPE OF DRILL: Pass protection blocking
NAME OF DRILL: Piedmont-pad
TO BE USED BY: Offensive Linemen
PURPOSE: To teach proper footwork and balance while blocking for the passer
SET UP:

1. Pair off players.

2. Designate one as the pass blocker and one as the rusher (Diagram 3-33).
3. The blocker will start in a three-point stance, the rusher in an upright stance.

Diagram 3-33.

Instructions:

1. On the signal from the coach the blocker will set up in his pass blocking position with his feet chopping.
2. The defensive man, in an upright position will use a forearm shiver and take three definite hits to the shoulder pads of the blocker.
3. After each hit the blocker will recoil and be in position for the next hit.
4. The defensive man should try to push the offensive blocker back.

Coaching points:

1. A yard stripe should separate the two men and they should stay on their own side.
2. The blocker should protect the ground he is standing on.
3. The defensive man can move right or left after the first skill has been mastered.
4. The defensive man becomes the offensive man and the offensive man becomes the defensive man.

TYPE OF DRILL: Pass blocking drill
NAME OF DRILL: Push-and-pull
TO BE USED BY: Offensive Blockers
PURPOSE: To teach balance and footwork for the offensive blocker

SET UP:

1. Players pair off.
2. A group of three is desirable (Diagram 3-34).

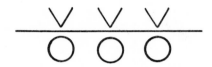

Diagram 3-34.

Instructions:

1. Offensive blocker is in a three-point stance and comes to a pass-protection position on the command of the coach.
2. Defensive man is in an upright stance.
3. The defensive man grabs the jersey of the blocker and pushes or pulls him off balance.
4. The blocker keeps his feet chopping and tries to control his ground.

Coaching points:

1. The coach should observe the blocker for position.
2. The defensive man should be warned that this is a drill and that he cannot grab a jersey in a game. This is for drill purposes only.

TYPE OF DRILL: Pass blocking
NAME OF DRILL: Lovers-lane
TO BE USED BY: Offensive Linemen
PURPOSE: To practice pass protection and to teach the blocker to stay with his man
SET UP:

1. Set up two dummies, lying on their side, two yards apart.
2. Set up one rusher and one blocker.

3. Use one lineman to simulate the quarterback.
4. Set up two of three of these groups.
5. The rusher becomes the blocker after each drill is completed (Diagram 3-35).

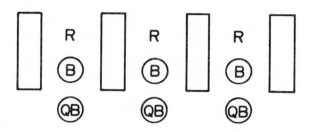

Diagram 3-35.

Instructions:

1. The rusher and the blocker are two yards apart.
2. The quarterback is about 3 yards back.
3. The rusher will use an air dummy or arm shield. Later this drill will become live.
4. On the signal from the coach, the rusher tries to get to the quarterback.
5. The drill is concluded when the rusher gets to the quarterback or the coach stops the drill because it has taken more than five seconds.

Coaching points:

1. This drill becomes very competitive.
2. The coach will be able to find his best pass rusher and his best pass blocker.
3. The coach moves from one group to another.

TYPE OF DRILL: Blocking
NAME OF DRILL: Drop-back-pass-protection
TO BE USED BY: Offensive Linemen
PURPOSE: To teach how to form a pocket for the drop back passer, not allowing a rush to come from the inside

SET UP:

1. Pair off players in groups of four.

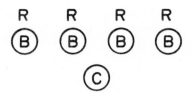

Diagram 3-36.

2. Coach stands 5–7 yards behind the offensive linemen (Diagram 3-36).
3. The coach will give the starting count and the blocker will use pocket protection.

Instructions:

1. Approach:
   A. Take a short step backwards with the inside foot, then a longer step back with the outside foot.
   B. While doing this, turn slightly to the inside remembering that the inside gap must be protected.
   C. After the second step backwards, you should be in a good football position ready to strike a blow.
   D. Keep feet chugging.
2. Making and maintaining contact:
   A. Look at the man to be blocked, make him come to you. When he is close enough, spring and make contact keeping your head up.
   B. After contact is made and the charge of the offensive man has been stopped, you then take a step back, regain your good football position and make contact again.
   C. At all times you must force the defensive man to the outside.
3. Follow through:
   A. When you see that you can no longer stay in front of the defensive man, due to his position, you try to drive him

with a reverse shoulder, getting your head between the rusher and the quarterback. Drive him out of the pocket.

B. As your last resort you can slide into a crab block.

C. At all times stay in the crab position and work your feet around to force your opponent to the outside, thus keeping him away from the passer.

Coaching points:

1. As this is designed as an offensive blocking drill, have the defensive man make a hard charge toward the passer. Later the defensive man can use his hands to pull the blocker off balance.
2. The drill should be started with the defensive man charging while carrying a light air dummy.
3. If the defensive man does get to the inside then the blocker should drive him into the middle.

TYPE OF DRILL: Blocking
NAME OF DRILL: Fundamentals-of-pass-blocking
TO BE USED BY: Offensive Linemen
PURPOSE: To teach proper form in pass blocking
SET UP:

1. Players pair off, designate one as the pass blocker and one as the pass rusher.
2. Players start in a three-point stance.
3. On the signal from the coach, the pass blocker will protect the passer (the coach) for at least five seconds.
4. The blocker becomes the rusher and the rusher becomes the blocker (Diagram 3-37).

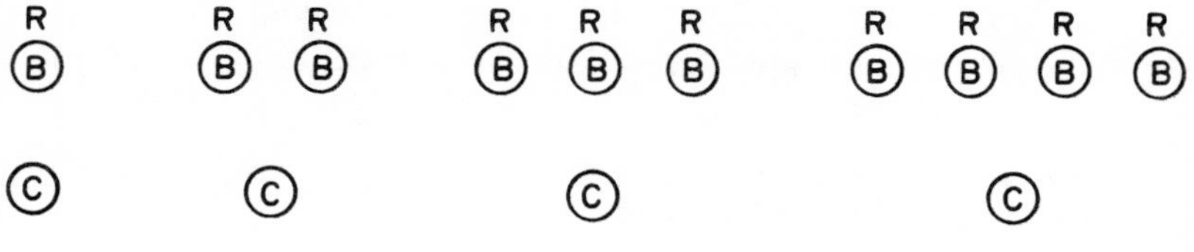

Diagram 3-37.

Instructions:

1. From the three-point stance, blocker will slide or set to a balanced position, head up, shoulders square, tail down, legs flexed, feet about shoulder width apart, weight on ball of the feet.
2. Elbows should be held into the sides (a boxer's position) to minimize the area that the defender might grab.
3. The blocker steps up into the opponent as he charges forward. The blocker's eyes should be aimed at the numbers, keeping eyes open and directly focused on the target. The thrust of the blow should go up into opponent, rather than forward. Never get over extended.
4. After each hit, recover quickly into the hitting position, taking away the defender's approach to the quarterback. Blocker must make the second move before the opponent's second move.
5. Keep square to the opponent, sliding one way or the other to position yourself in front of him (between opponent and quarterback).
6. Be ready to absorb punishment, keeping patience and proper body position.
7. Keep opponent off balance by cutting him occasionally but you must recover before he does.
8. Adjust your blocking to the type of defensive charge.
9. Keep feet churning at all times.

Coaching points:

1. Start the drill with the blocker facing the coach. Coach checks his position and initial movement.
2. Add a rusher with a light dummy.
3. Go live one on one.
4. Progress until you have a four on four situation.
5. Add a real live quarterback if one is available.

TYPE OF DRILL: Pass blocking
NAME OF DRILL: Six-on-six
TO BE USED BY: Offensive Linemen
PURPOSE: To practice pass blocking techniques against various defensive set ups

SET UP:

1. Set up six offensive linemen and six defensive linemen plus a quarterback (Diagram 3-38).

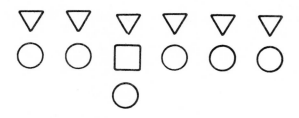

Diagram 3-38.

Instructions:

1. Defensive men may line up in any position, i.e. head, gap, backer and they react to the move of the quarterback.
2. The quarterback calls a play in the huddle:
   A. Drop-back pass.
   B. Sprint-out pass right or left.
   C. Roll-out pass right or left.
3. The offensive blockers use their rules for the type of passing game called.
4. The defensive players *do not* tackle the quarterback.

Coaching points:

1. The progression would be for the coach to start with the proper technique for each type of pass.
2. Once the skills are mastered, the coach should install his pass blocking rules for each type of pass. If only one type is used then that is the only one called.
3. The quarterback will change the count and even run a QB sneak to keep the defense honest. A back or two may be added to show a running play to also keep the defense honest.

TYPE OF DRILL: Pass protection
NAME OF DRILL: Progression-pass-protection

TO BE USED BY: Linemen
PURPOSE: To teach and review the basic pass protec-
                tion techniques
SET UP:

   1. The drill progresses from a one-on-one situation, to a half
      line set up, then finally to a full line set up (Diagram
      3-39).

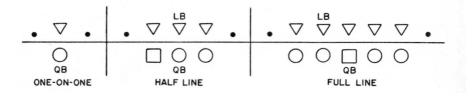

Diagram 3-39.

Instructions:

   1. The first part of the drill is used to teach a pass blocker the
      fundamentals. The rusher can do anything he wants inside
      the boundaries in order to get to the quarterback.
   2. The idea of the drill is for the blocker to keep the rusher
      out for an allotted amount of time.
   3. The drill should be taught for form first, making sure that
      the necessary fundamentals are understood. Then progress
      to a live situation.
   4. The second phase is identical to phase one only using a half
      team. The coach may check splits, set-up, blocking areas
      and all the techniques previously mentioned.
   5. The purpose of phase three is to incorporate the entire line-
      blocking looking for the same results as above.

Coaching points:

   1. By teaching the part method in the progression drill the
      protector can visualize what the end result should be.
   2. In the beginning the protectors can walk through the drill
      in order to see the whole picture.
   3. When the half line or the full line is incorporated it is

necessary to explain the splits. A split may vary with the individual's capabilities.

4. The rule of thumb is that no one breaks the cup to the inside. Rushers must go to the outside.
5. The blockers are defending areas and not individual men. They set up and let the defense come. In this way they can see the defense unfold and pick up any stunts.
6. The coach should stress body control and movement of the feet with the knees bent at all times.

TYPE OF DRILL: Pass blocking
NAME OF DRILL: McQueary-blitz-blocking
TO BE USED BY: Offensive Linemen
PURPOSE: To teach lineman to react to a linebacker over him

SET UP:

1. Set up a passer, blocker, linebacker and a defensive end.
2. Defensive men use light bags or arm shields.

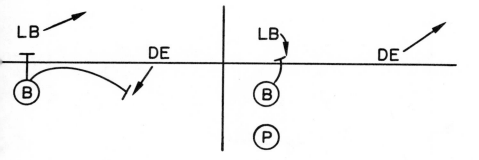

Diagram 3-40.

Instructions:

1. Coach designates which defensive man will rush the passer.
2. Blocker must recognize whether or not the linebacker is blitzing, if he does he blocks him.

3. If the linebacker does not blitz, the offensive lineman will move out to cut off the outside rusher (Diagram 3-40).

Coaching points:

1. Always protect the inside first.
2. Maintain good hitting position at all times.
3. Keep shoulders square with defensive man.
4. Blocker should get an inside-out position on the outside rusher.

TYPE OF DRILL: Blocking
NAME OF DRILL: McQueary-screen-pass
TO BE USED BY: Linemen
PURPOSE: To teach linemen correct timing in releasing for the screen
SET UP:

1. Set up a skeletal formation, center, guard, tackle, three defensive linemen, and three defensive secondary men.

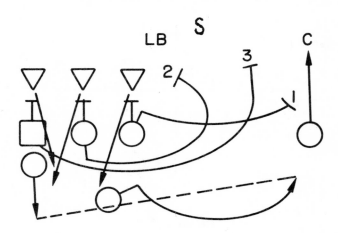

Diagram 3-41.

Instructions:

1. Defensive personnel use light dummies or arm shields.
2. Rushers try to get penetration.

3. Offensive linemen get two or three hits before releasing.
4. Defensive backs react to the receiver (screen man).
5. Offensive linemen leave when the tackle leaves and block accordingly: First blocker out, block corner back.
   Second blocker out, looks to the inside anticipating pressure from the linebacker.
   Third blocker is assigned as a "personal protector" and block the most dangerous man (Diagram 3-41).

Coaching points:

1. Blockers should be made conscious of staying behind the line of scrimmage. Receiver can aid this by yelling "Go" while the ball is in the air.
2. Blockers should attempt to release the man at the line of scrimmage to the outside. Long path to the passer.

TYPE OF DRILL: Blocking
NAME OF DRILL: Blocking-a-stunting-defense
TO BE USED BY: Linemen
PURPOSE: To teach linemen to block against a stunting defense

SET UP:

1. This drill has four set ups: the stack, the scissors, crab and gap.

Instructions:

I. The Stack:

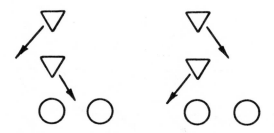

Diagram 3-42.

A. Four linemen are set up. Two offensive linemen and two defensive linemen in a stack position.
B. The offensive blockers will block area rather than man.
C. The defensive men vary their charge: down-man right and up-man left or down-man left and up-man right (Diagram 3-42).

Coaching points:

1. Stress stepping with the inside foot, or the foot nearest the hole area, and blocking the man that arrives in that gap.

II. The Scissors:

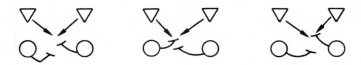

Diagram 3-43.

A. Four men are set up. Two offensive men and two defensive men.
B. The offensive lineman must keep his head up and read this stunt quickly.
C. As his number moves right or left he must stay with his number and try to stop any penetration and move him laterally by the hole. This is an important cross block by offensive linemen (Diagram 3-43).

III. Gap Drill:

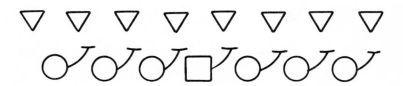

Diagram 3-44.

   A. Defensive men are placed in the gaps between the offensive linemen.

   B. The defense tries to get penetration.

   C. The offensive blocker must get his head in front of the defensive man (Diagram 3-44).

Coaching points:

1. If the defense is going to penetrate he must go through the blockers head.

IV. Crab Drill:

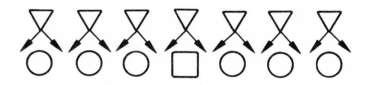

Diagram 3-45.

   A. Defensive linemen are head up two or three feet off the ball.

   B. The coach stands behind the offense and gives the direction of charge to the defense.

   C. On the snap the offense must fire out and stay with the defense (Diagram 3-45).

Coaching points:

1. The important thing is for the blocker to minimize the penetration.

CHAPTER FOUR

Winning Drills for Pulling and Trapping Linemen

When one thinks of pulling he immediately thinks of trapping but this is only part of the pulling lineman's duties. In addition to the trap block the pulling lineman must be able to pull and lead for the sweep, pull for the quick pitch, pull to influence a defensive lineman and in some cases pull to protect for the passer.

If the offense incorporates the pulling lineman then this becomes one of the most important assignments in the offensive structure.

The stance, the steps, the path, the short trap, the long trap all are part of positions that a pulling lineman must learn.

The initial move and the quickness in which the lineman gets to the point of attack are the most important elements of the pulling assignment.

Several drills are listed so that the coach may be able to drill on the various techniques required of the pulling lineman.

TYPE OF DRILL: Pulling
NAME OF DRILL: Correct-step
TO BE USED BY: Offensive Linemen
PURPOSE: To teach the linemen the correct steps in pulling for the quick trap
SET UP: All linemen line up facing the coach

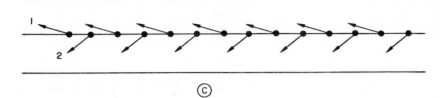

Diagram 4-1.

Instructions:

1. Linemen will assume an offensive stance.
2. The coach will designate which way the linemen are to pull, either right or left.
3. The coach will say, "right one." On the command "one," the linemen will pivot on his left foot and simultaneously step diagonally, about six inches to his right with his right foot.
4. The linemen should grab grass with his inside hand (left) and at this point look like a sprinter. The coach will check the players in this position.
5. On command "two," the lineman will step across the line with his left foot. The coach will check the position at this point.
6. On the command "three," the players will charge about three yards. They should be headed diagonally up field (Diagram 4-1).
7. On the command "left," the above process is reversed.

Coaching points:

1. Weight should always be on the inside foot so that the lineman can move his outside foot quickly and be ready to shove off with the inside foot.

TYPE OF DRILL: Pulling and trapping
NAME OF DRILL: 1-2-3-Trap
TO BE USED BY: Guards and Tackles
PURPOSE: To teach the pulling lineman the propei
                 techniques for trapping a defensive lineman
                 who may be 1 on the line, 2 one step across
                 the line, or 3 in the offensive backfield

SET UP:

1. Set up two linemen in their normal position on the line of scrimmage.
2. Set up three dummies, with holders, simulating a defensive lineman.
3. The dummies are numbered 1-2-3.
4. The coach stands in front of the linemen.

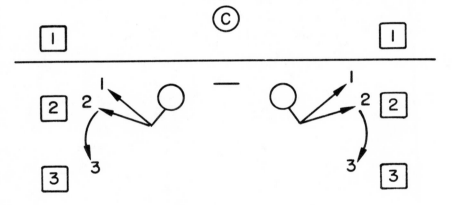

Diagram 4-2.

Instructions:

1. The coach will work one side at a time.
2. The coach will give the starting count. Once the lineman has started to pull, the coach will give the designated number of the dummy to hit.
3. The pulling lineman will always head for dummy number one, and then proceed to the number called.
4. When pulling right, the trapper will use his right shoulder on dummies one and two and his left shoulder on number

three, which will be a reverse shoulder block. The procedure is reversed when going left (Diagram 4-2).

Coaching points:

The coach should check proper pulling techniques and make sure that the trapper is under control when he approaches the dummy.

TYPE OF DRILL: Pulling and trapping
NAME OF DRILL: Trapping-the-board
TO BE USED BY: Pulling Linemen
PURPOSE: To develop correct techniques in executing the first steps in a trap block
SET UP:

1. Set up two lines facing the coach.
2. Set up two boards (2″ × 12″ × 6′ long).
3. Set up a dummy and a holder on each board.

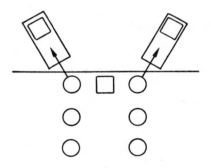

Diagram 4-3.

Instructions:

1. Players line up in a three-point stance.
2. On the command from the coach, the players pull and straddle the boards then block the dummy off the board.
3. Proper steps should be taken while approaching the board.
4. Players rotate left and right. The puller becomes the dummy holder and the dummy holder the puller (Diagram 4-3).

Coaching points:

1. Stress good stance, wide base. All weight on the inside foot, push off inside foot, throw arm, stay low, grab grass with inside hand.
2. Players stay low and approach the dummy under control.
3. The board may be moved to position two or position three (see Correct Step drill).

TYPE OF DRILL: Pull and lead
NAME OF DRILL: Cal
TO BE USED BY: Pulling Linemen
PURPOSE: To check pulling linemen for speed, agility, balance and hitting
SET UP:

1. Set up two groups of linemen. They should be paired by position. This makes for better competition.
2. Set up six markers, two dummies with holders as diagrammed.
3. The coach faces the drill with a stop-watch.

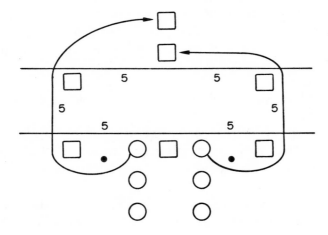

Diagram 4-4.

Instructions:

1. On the coach's signal the two linemen in front of the line will pull to their outside, one will pull right and one will pull left.
2. The linemen will cut around the markers and hit the dummies (Diagram 4-4).
3. The lineman that pulls left with his left shoulder and the lineman that pulls right will hit with his right shoulder.
4. Coach will give the time of the first man to hit.

Coaching points:

1. This drill becomes very competitive. It will decide the fastest pulling lineman.
2. Coach should stress a proper hitting position when the linemen round the last marker before hitting the dummy.
3. The lineman will hold the dummy he hits, and the dummy holder will get in line. Players should alternate so that they pull left and right.

TYPE OF DRILL: Pull and Lead
NAME OF DRILL: Funnel
TO BE USED BY: Pulling Linemen
PURPOSE: To check pulling linemen for speed, agility and balance while blocking downfield
SET UP:

1. Set up two groups of linemen in offensive guard's position.
2. Set up four markers and two dummies with holders.
   A. Two markers are placed at each end of the line of scrimmage five yards from the center and one yard from the line.
   B. Two markers are placed on the defensive side of the line directly in front of the pulling linemen and three yards off the line.
   C. Two dummies with holders are placed directly in front of the pulling linemen five yards off the line.

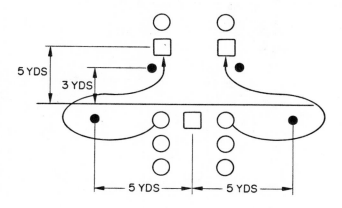

Diagram 4-5.

Instructions:

1. On the signal from the coach, the linemen pull to the outside, one lineman pulls right and one lineman pulls left.
2. The linemen pull around the first marker, cut inside of the middle markers and shoulder block the dummies (Diagram 4-5).
3. The coach will time all players with a stop watch.

Coaching points:

1. This drill is similar to the Call Drill with the exception that it gives the player a feeling of cutting up-field to lead the play.
2. The blocker becomes the dummy holder and the dummy holder returns to the line of pulling linemen.

TYPE OF DRILL: Pulling
NAME OF DRILL: Around-the-hat
TO BE USED BY: Pulling Linemen
PURPOSE: To develop techniques of pulling, speed and quickness
SET UP:

1. Set up two lines of players.

2. Set up two markers on each side as diagrammed.
3. Coach faces players.

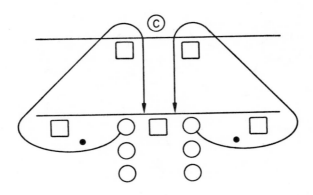

Diagram 4-6.

Instructions:

1. Players line up in a three-point stance, side by side.
2. On the command of the coach, players pull around the markers using correct lead pull techniques.
3. Players rotate to the end of the line, changing lines each time so that they will have a chance to pull right and left (Diagram 4-6).
4. Coach times players with a stop watch.

Coaching points:

1. This drill can be set up as a competitive drill to see who the fastest pulling lineman is.
2. Markers may be placed at different spots to emphasize various pulling techniques.

TYPE OF DRILL: Trap and fill
NAME OF DRILL: Cross
TO BE USED BY: Guards, Tackles and Centers
PURPOSE: To teach the linemen how to pull and fill for the quick trap

SET UP:

1. Set up two lines of players in front of two standing dummies with holders.
2. Set up two groups in like manner.
3. Coach will station himself between the groups.

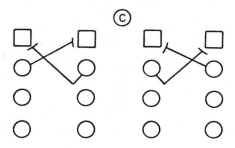

Diagram 4-7.

Instructions:

1. One group will have the man on the left pull left and block the dummy with his left shoulder. The man on the right will use a fill-in type block, i.e. near-foot, near-shoulder, reverse shoulder to a crab.
2. The other group will have the man on the right pull right and block the dummy with his right shoulder, the man on the left will use a fill-in type block, i.e. near-foot, near-shoulder or reverse shoulder to a crab (Diagram 4-7).
3. The player that hits the dummy will become the dummy holder and the dummy holder will become the blocker.
4. Players rotate until they have pulled and trapped left and right and used a left and right fill in block.
5. The two groups may use the same starting count or the coach may move from one group to another.

TYPE OF DRILL: Pulling and trapping
NAME OF DRILL: Guarding-the-line
TO BE USED BY: Offensive Linemen

PURPOSE: To find out who is the best pulling and trapping lineman, also to see who is the strongest upon contact and to find out who can stay with their man the longest

SET UP:

1. Set up one group of linemen, holding dummies on the five yard line.
2. Set up a group of blockers, at right angles to the dummies, on the ten yard line.

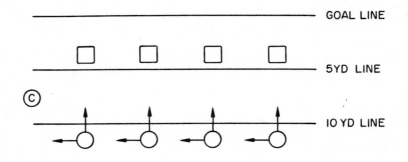

Diagram 4-8.

Instructions:

1. On the signal from the coach, the linemen pull right (or left) and try to drive the dummies into the end zone.
2. The men holding the dummies resist the pulling linemen and try not to get pushed into the end zone (Diagram 4-8).
3. For a little competition, after everyone has had a few hits, take the player out who drives the dummy into the end zone. See who is first and see who is last. Very interesting!!

Coaching points:

1. This is the type of drill that should be used at the end of practice.
2. The coach should be on the look-out for bad habits, as the

blockers are more concerned in driving the man into the end zone than they are with form.

3. The coach can very easily pick out his best "trapper."

TYPE OF DRILL: Pulling, trapping, filling drill
NAME OF DRILL: Combination-drill—5-on-5
TO BE USED BY: Offensive Line (excluding Ends)
PURPOSE: To review all the fundamentals of pulling, trapping and filling

SET UP:

1. Set up the interior offensive line, center, two guards and two tackles.
2. Set up a five-man defensive line (Diagram 4-9).

Diagram 4-9.

Instructions:

1. The basic drill is to have the guards pull to the outside, the tackles fill down, and the center work on a man head-up or in the linebacker position.
2. From this basic set any combination may be used including the post and lead block. For a change-up, the offensive line should just fire out on a man-on-man charge to keep the defense honest.
3. Players should rotate so that they pull and trap left and right as well as fill left and right.

Coaching points:

1. The coach may want to elaborate on this drill. Using his own line blocking. However this particular drill is designed to work on the basic fundamentals of pulling, trapping, filling.

TYPE OF DRILL: Pulling
NAME OF DRILL: Pull-and-seal
TO BE USED BY: Offensive Linemen
PURPOSE: To combine the fill-in or seal block with
                                     sweep pulling
SET UP:

1. Set up four offensive linemen.
2. Set up two down linemen and two linebackers.
3. Defensive personnel start with dummies or arm shields.

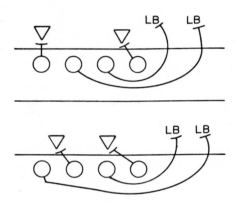

Diagram 4-10.

Instructions:

1. On the signal from the coach, two linemen will pull and two linemen will seal to the inside.
2. The first man around the corner will block the first man that shows.
3. The second man around the corner will block the free linebacker (Diagram 4-10).
4. The coach will vary the men who will pull to keep the defense honest.

Coaching points:

1. The coach should have the defensive men play it straight until the drill is mastered and then he should let them go.

2. The pulling linemen should gain depth and be under control as they round the corner.
3. The down linemen should vary their blocks.
4. The coach will huddle the offensive blockers and tell them what type of blocking he wants.

TYPE OF DRILL: Pulling
NAME OF DRILL: Quick-pitch
TO BE USED BY: Offensive Linemen
PURPOSE: To teach proper techniques of pulling for the quick pitch or sweep
SET UP:

1. Set up players on the line of scrimmage in their relative positions, i.e. guards and tackles.
2. Set up four defensive men with dummies. Two down linemen and two corner backs.
3. Set up two markers in the offensive backfield, two yards deep.

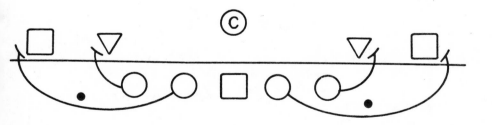

Diagram 4-11.

Instructions:

1. Offensive players line up in a three-point stance.
2. On the signal from the coach, the guards pull deep around the markers, square up and block the corner backs.
3. The tackles use a reach block on the defensive men who are playing to their outside (Diagram 4-11).
4. Blocker becomes dummy holder, dummy holder becomes the blocker.

5. The tackles also pull and the guards use a reach block on the man to their outside. Note: move the defensive man to the outside shoulder of the guards for this phase of the drill.

Coaching points:

1. Stress pushing off the inside foot, throwing arm in the direction of pull and gain ground.

TYPE OF DRILL: Trap, lead and cut-off
NAME OF DRILL: 3-on-3-trap
TO BE USED BY: Centers and Guards
PURPOSE: To teach the guards the quick trap, to teach the guard to pull and lead around the corner and to teach the center the cut off block

SET UP:

1. Set up three offensive men, two guards and a center.
2. Set up three defensive men, two down linemen and one linebacker (Diagram 4-12).

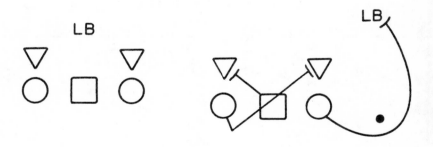

Diagram 4-12.   *Diagram 4-13.*

Instructions:

1. Left guard pulls right and traps first man past the center. Right guard pulls and blocks linebacker. Center blocks to his left (Diagram 4-13).

2. Right guard pulls left and traps first man past center. Left guard pulls left and blocks linebacker. Center blocks right (Diagram 4-14).

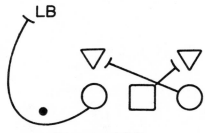

Diagram 4-14.

3. Both guards block straight ahead. Center blocks linebacker. Note: this keeps the defense honest (Diagram 4-15).

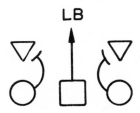

Diagram 4-15.

Coaching points:

1. This drill may be used against light dummies or arm shields but it is best when it is live.
2. The coach may use any combination of blocks he so desires.

TYPE OF DRILL: Pulling
NAME OF DRILL: Sweep
TO BE USED BY: Offensive guards and tackles
PURPOSE: To develop the correct pattern for running the sweep
SET UP:

1. Set up two lines, designate them as the ON guard and the OFF guard.

2. Set up one dummy and holder to simulate a defensive end crossing the line of scrimmage.
3. Set up one dummy to simulate a linebacker filling the sweep hole (Diagram 4-16).

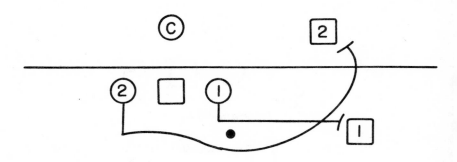

Diagram 4-16.

Instructions:

1. Offensive players line up in a three-point stance at the line of scrimmage.
2. On the signal from the coach, both offensive linemen pull.
3. The on-lineman blocks the defensive end out.
4. The off-lineman blocks the linebacker who is filling the sweep hole.
5. The linemen hold the dummy they hit, and the dummy holders get in line.
6. Players should alternate so that they have an opportunity to be both the "on" and "off" guard.
7. This drill should be run to the left also.

Coaching points:

1. Coach should stress proper pulling techniques, proper depth, good football position upon contact.

TYPE OF DRILL: Trapping
NAME OF DRILL: Trap-vs-Stunts
TO BE USED BY: Offensive Linemen
PURPOSE: To work on the trap block vs stunts

SET UP:

1. Set up an offensive interior line, center, guards and tackles.
2. Set up a defensive line, three down-men and two line-backers.
3. The defense may vary its stunts.

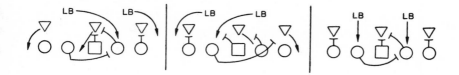

Diagram 4-17.

Instructions:

1. Both teams huddle, the offense calls a trap play and the defense calls a stunt. Linebackers fire; slant right; slant left or any combination (Diagram 4-17).
2. To start the drill, however, the defense should play it straight until all assignments are mastered.
3. The coach should also "walk and talk" the assignments vs the stunts so that the offensive players will know how to handle them.
4. The defense should start the drill with light dummies or arm shields before going live.

Coaching points:

1. The offense should block straight ahead at times to keep the defense honest.
2. A backfield may be added to this drill to make it more realistic.
3. The coach should have two groups going and move from one to the other. One group can trap left and one group can trap right.

TYPE OF DRILL: Pulling
NAME OF DRILL: Pull-and-cut

TO BE USED BY: Pulling Linemen
PURPOSE: To check proper pulling techniques and to teach a pulling lineman how to pull and cut up-field for a linebacker

SET UP:

1. Two guards line up in their normal position.
2. A dummy and holder are placed to simulate defensive ends.
3. A dummy and holder are placed to simulate linebackers.
4. The above situations are set up on both sides.

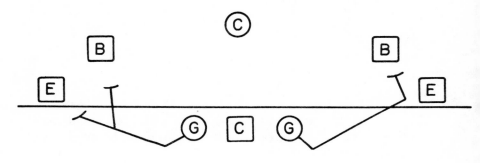

Diagram 4-18.

Instructions:

1. The linemen assume a proper offensive stance.
2. On the coach's command, both linemen pull, one pulls right and the other pulls left.
3. After they have taken their initial steps, the coach will call, "End" or "Backer." The pulling lineman will block the man called (Diagram 4-18).
4. The blocker becomes the dummy holder, the holder the blocker.

Coaching points:

1. The coach, after checking the initial pulling motion, will check to see if the lineman is in position to make the block on the end, and to see that he does not break his stride if the backer is called.

TYPE OF DRILL: Pull and trap

NAME OF DRILL: Trapping-the-Two-Man-Sled
TO BE USED BY: Pulling Linemen
PURPOSE: To stress good form in pulling out of the line, plus good hitting techniques
SET UP:

1. Set up a two-on-one situation at right angles to the sled (Diagram 4-19).
2. Set up two offensive men and one defensive man (Diagram 4-20).

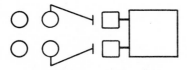

TWO MEN TRAPPING THE SLED

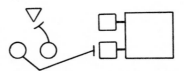

ONE MAN FILLING, ONE MAN TRAPPING

Diagram 4-19.   *Diagram 4-20.*

Instructions:

1. This drill may start with all men trapping the sled. Have linemen facing each other, one pulls left and one pulls right trapping with their corresponding shoulder.
2. Once all linemen have trapped the sled a few times, the coach can have one man use a fill block on a defensive lineman and one man pull and trap the sled.
3. The coach may set up any combinations of the above, depending on the particular emphasis he wants to cover in this particular drill.

Coaching points:

1. The idea of the drill is to insure good form. The coach should not be too concerned with the "hit" at this point.
2. The coach should have someone on the sled, otherwise the drill moves too much and gets out of proportion.

CHAPTER FIVE

Winning Drills for the Defensive Line

Defensive football is a game of reactions. It brings out the natural instincts of a ball player. Building confidence in the player's mind so that all defensive maneuvers are sound, is probably the most important item in teaching defensive skills.

Simplicity seems to be the key word in football and this can only be obtained through proper teaching methods and by constant repetition of the skills involved.

Building pride in defensive line play must also become an important part in teaching defensive football.

Defensive line drills will vary with the type of defense that is employed but in developing these drills there are some basic principles that must be followed.

MOVE ON THE BALL

Interior linemen should be taught to react to movement; either movement of the ball or movement of the offensive blocker.

STRIKE A BLOW

Linemen must be taught to strike a blow on movement.

NEUTRALIZE THE OFFENSIVE CHARGE

The interior lineman in striking a blow must be able to neutralize and disengage the offensive blocker and be under control so that he can react to the play.

PROTECT THE TERRITORY

This should be the creed of all interior linemen. He must learn to do "first things first."

LOCATE THE BALL CARRIER

Linemen must know where the ball is before leaving his own territory. By following the above principles the lineman should always be in the correct position.

NEVER GO AROUND A BLOCKER

Linemen should never go around a blocker in order to get to the ball carrier because he will leave his position unguarded. He must react to the pressure of the blocker and either go through him, over him or under him.

PURSUE OR CHASE THE BALL CARRIER

Good pursuit or chase is essential to successful defensive play. Depending on the defensive technique that is used, the linemen will either chase or pursue the ball carrier.

GANG TACKLING

All defensive linemen must be responsible for either assisting in or making the tackle.

The following drills are designed to accomplish the above principles of line play.

TYPE OF DRILL: Defensive
NAME OF DRILL: Stance

TO BE USED BY: Defensive Linemen
PURPOSE: To work on the fundamentals of a good stance
SET UP:

1. Set up defensive linemen on a yard stripe facing the coach (Diagram 5-1).

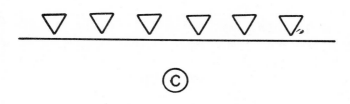

Diagram 5-1.

Instructions:

1. Coach works on both a three-point stance and a four-point stance.
2. Coach moves ball and checks defensive movement; players take one step.
3. Coach moves hand and checks defensive movement; players take one step.

Coaching points:

1. Coach checks for the following:
   A. Good base, feet shoulder width apart, toe heel alignment.
   B. Knees flexed, butt sucked up under feet, back parallel to ground.
   C. Hand(s) down about five inches in front of shoulders. Head and eyes up.
2. A defensive lineman should:
   A. Key the down hand of the offensive man and the ball.
   B. Strike a blow on movement (control, neutralize, disengage).
   C. Be able to move in any direction.

3. Three things for a defensive lineman to remember:
   A. No opponent may control your knees.
   B. Work from a low plane to a high plane.
   C. Play yourself off the blocker.
4. Responsibilities of a defensive lineman:
   A. Alignment, block protection, control, locate ball, pursue or chase, tackle.

TYPE OF DRILL: Defensive
NAME OF DRILL: Step
TO BE USED BY: Defensive Linemen
PURPOSE: To teach defensive linemen how to keep from over-extending
SET UP:

1. Defensive linemen line up on a line facing the coach (Diagram 5-2).

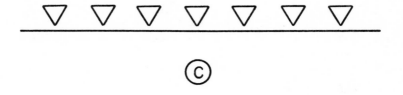

Diagram 5-2.

Instructions:

1. Coach will call numbers 1, 2, 3 and players will step on each number.
2. On number one, the lineman will step with his back foot and raise his corresponding forearm.
3. On number two, the lineman will step with his front foot and raise his corresponding forearm.
4. On number three, the defensive lineman will "square up," getting himself in a ready position to ward off the indie trap, play the man head up and also be ready to play the isolation block.

Coaching points:

1. This is a "walk and talk" type drill. The coach should remind the defensive players of their responsibilities as they take each step.
2. The coach should make sure that the feet are parallel, back arched, legs flexed, head up, when the players reach the third count. They should be in a hit position and ready for any kind of an offensive maneuver.

TYPE OF DRILL: Defensive reaction drill
NAME OF DRILL: Eagle
TO BE USED BY: Defensive Linemen
PURPOSE: To teach reaction and to learn to fight pressure

SET UP:

1. Set up two offensive men with light dummies or arm shields.
2. Set up one defensive man in a four-point stance facing the two offensive men (Diagram 5-3).
3. Set up as many groups as feasible.

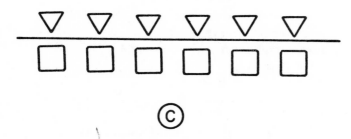

Diagram 5-3.

Instructions:

1. On the signal from the coach, the right offensive man fires out into the defensive man.
2. The defensive man reacts with a left forearm lift and returns to his original position.
3. Once the defensive man is in position, the left offensive man fires out and the defensive man reacts with a right

forearm lift and returns to his original position.

4. This continues until the defensive man has reacted two or three times to each man.

5. This drill is best when live, but the coach must keep it under control and time the blocking of the offensive linemen so that the defensive man has a chance to recover.

6. If the drill is live the offensive men use a shoulder block on the defensive man.

Coaching points:

1. The drill seems to work better if the coach tells the offense when to hit. This gives the defensive man a chance to regroup and be ready for the next hit.

TYPE OF DRILL: Defensive
NAME OF DRILL: Forearm-Lift-Technique
TO BE USED BY: Defensive Lineman
PURPOSE: To teach linemen how to use a forearm lift
SET UP:

1. Linemen pair off, one man holding a dummy and one man in a defensive stance (Diagram 5-4).

2. The coach may use as many groups as feasible.

3. The player holding the dummy should tilt the dummy forward to simulate an offensive lineman.

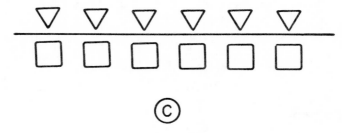

Diagram 5-4.

Instructions:

1. On the coach's signal the dummy holders will tilt the dummy forward.

2. The defensive man will use a forearm lift (alternate arms) placing his corresponding shoulder into the dummy as he hits.
3. The defensive man should step with the same foot that he is hitting with, i.e. right arm and shoulder step with right foot, left forearm and left shoulder step with his left foot.
4. After initial contact the defensive man should be squared up, feet parallel, back arched, head up, and be ready to move right or left.
5. The off arm of the defensive man should be placed high on the dummy simulating the hand on the opponent's shoulder pads.

Coaching points:

1. The drill may be started by the defensive man hitting the dummy without anyone holding it (the dummy holder can just hold the top to balance it). The defensive man uses his forearm and tries to flip the dummy over. This teaches the proper method of the lift. Obviously this is easier accomplished with a light dummy.

TYPE OF DRILL: Defensive
NAME OF DRILL: Reaction
TO BE USED BY: Defensive Linemen
PURPOSE: To teach down-linemen to react to various moves of an offensive lineman
SET UP:

1. Players pair off, one yard on either side of a yard stripe.
2. Designate one line as offense and one line as defense.

Instructions:

1. The coach will stand behind the defense and signal to the offensive linemen the type of move that he desires.
2. The offensive linemen will take one step in the direction of the move.
3. The defensive lineman will take one step and react to the offensive man's move (Diagram 5-5).

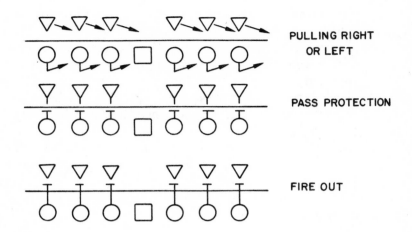

Diagram 5-5.

4. This is a non-contact drill, the defensive man will just simulate his action.
5. Various types of moves can be made: Fire out block; pull
   right or left; pass protection, etc.

Coaching points:

1. Once all the moves have been made the coach will switch
   the lines so that every lineman has a chance to react.
2. Players should use proper form and use exact execution of
   the techniques.
3. Do not let the players get sloppy in this drill.

TYPE OF DRILL: Defensive
NAME OF DRILL: Reaction
TO BE USED BY: Defensive Linemen
PURPOSE: To teach down-linemen to react to the vari-
                              ous moves an offensive lineman will make
SET UP:

1. Players pair off, one yard on either side of a yard stripe.
2. Designate one line as offense and one line as defense.

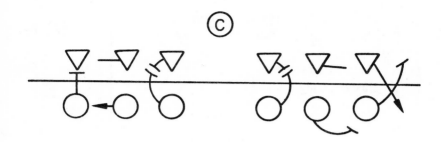

Diagram 5-6.

Instructions:

1. The coach will stand behind the defense and signal to the offensive linemen the type of move that he desires.
2. The offensive linemen will take one step in the direction of the move.
3. The defensive lineman will take one step and react to the offensive move (Diagram 5-6).
4. This is a non-contact drill, the defensive man will just simulate his action.
5. Various types of moves can be made: Straight ahead block; pull right or left; pass protection; downfield blocking.

Coaching points:

1. Once all the moves have been made the coach will switch the lines so that every lineman has a chance to react.
2. Players should use proper form and use exact execution of the techniques.
3. Do not let the players get sloppy in this drill.

TYPE OF DRILL: Defensive
NAME OF DRILL: Cluster
TO BE USED BY: Defensive Linemen
PURPOSE: To teach the defensive linemen to get across the line and to avoid "wrestling" with the blocker

SET UP:

1. Three players hold light dummies in a "cluster."
2. Place another dummy and holder five yards behind the cluster.
3. Place a defensive man in a four-point stance in front of the cluster (Diagram 5-7).

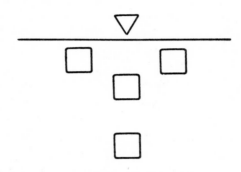

Diagram 5-7.

Instructions:

1. On the command from the coach, the defensive man, working from a four-point stance, tries to break through the "cluster" and tackle the dummy that is five yards behind the cluster.
2. The men holding the dummies apply pressure but let the man through.
3. The defensive man should reach the last dummy within three seconds.
4. Players rotate so that they all get a chance to break through.

Coaching points:

1. This drill gets very competitive and is best vs the dummies. It may be used live but has a tendency to get out of hand.
2. The coach is trying to get the defensive man off the hook and into the backfield. The defensive man gets a good workout while wrestling with the blockers but does not help the defense out. Actually, he is taking himself out of the play.

TYPE OF DRILL: Defensive Charge
NAME OF DRILL: Shooting-the-gap
TO BE USED BY: Defensive Linemen
PURPOSE: To teach defensive linemen to get across the line of scrimmage "under control" and be ready for the next resistance

SET UP:

1. Set up two groups of linemen with light dummies or arm shields facing the coach.
2. Have one defensive lineman in a defensive stance facing the blockers (Diagram 5-8).

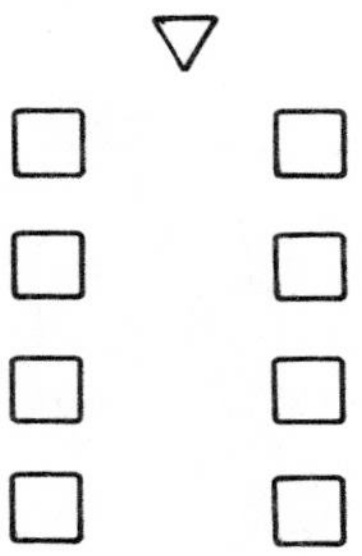

Diagram 5-8.

Instructions:

1. On the signal from the coach, the defensive lineman charge between the two blockers. The blockers exert pressure but let the defensive man through.
2. The defensive man regroups after he goes through the first two blockers and then tries to get through the next two.
3. He proceeds until he gets through three sets of blockers. He then sprints ten yards in a football position.

Coaching points:

1. This drill may be used live with the two blockers closing on the defensive man and giving him one good shoulder charge.

TYPE OF DRILL: Combination offensive and defensive

NAME OF DRILL: West Point
TO BE USED BY: Defensive Linemen (also may be used as an
                offensive drill)
PURPOSE: To teach defensive men to protect their area
                and react to the ball
SET UP:

1. Place four dummies on the ground, two yards apart.
2. Place an offensive lineman and a defensive lineman between
    the dummies.
3. Set up a quarterback and three backs (Diagram 5-9).
    (Linemen may be used with the coach acting as the quarter-
    back, but the drill is more realistic if a full backfield is
    used.)

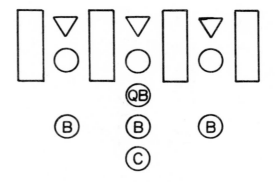

Diagram 5-9.

Instructions:

1. Offensive team huddles, quarterback calls the starting
    count.
2. All backs dive straight ahead, the quarterback hands off to
    one of the backs. One back becomes the ball carrier and the
    other two backs fake into the line and become blockers.
    The drill works best if the backs do not know who is to
    receive the ball.
3. Offensive blockers fire out and clear their area.
4. Defensive men protect their area, find the ball and make
    the tackle. There should be three defensive linemen around
    the ball on each play.

Coaching points:

1. The coach can make a game situation out of this drill. That is, he can start the drill on the 15 yard line and give the offense four plays to score. Points are awarded to the offense if they score, and to the defense if they hold them.

TYPE OF DRILL: Defensive line
NAME OF DRILL: Splitting-the-seam
TO BE USED BY: Down-defensive Linemen
PURPOSE: To practice breaking the double-team block
SET UP:

1. Set up two dummies with holders to simulate offensive line-men.
2. Set up one defensive man in a four-point stance (Diagram 5-10).
3. Set up as many groups as feasible.
4. This drill is best when used live, but should be started vs dummies or men wearing arm shields.

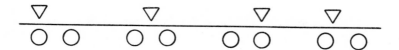

Diagram 5-10.

Instructions:

1. Defensive man tries to get across the line of scrimmage, protecting his area first, then trying to locate the ball.
2. Defensive man may do one of four things:
    A. Concentrate on either one of the offensive blockers and try to beat him.
    B. Use a "dip" charge (submarine), charging low, trying to get under the offensive blocker's charge.
    C. Knife through by turning his body edgewise in an attempt to split the seam and slide through the narrow opening. The defensive man uses his hands on one

blocker and his buttocks on the other.
  D. Use a double coordination movement. Line up in front
     of one opponent and on the first move direct your
     charge at the other blocker. The next move is back at
     the first opponent and then to cross the line.

Coaching points:

  1. Coach should emphasize that it is difficult for one man to
     beat two men unless one of the above techniques are used.
  2. Players rotate so that all become the defensive man.

TYPE OF DRILL: Defensive
NAME OF DRILL: Two-on-one
TO BE USED BY: Defensive Linemen
PURPOSE: To teach the down-defensive lineman to play
                 and react to the pressure of the offensive
                 blocker
SET UP:

  1. Set up groups of three linemen, five yards apart.
  2. Designate two linemen as offensive blockers and one line-
     man as a defensive man (Diagram 5-11).
  3. Coach stands behind the defensive man.

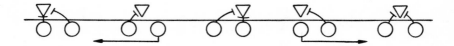

Diagram 5-11.

Instructions:

  1. Coach tells the offensive blockers the type of block to use.
     He does this by hand signals and has the following options:
     A. Both blockers fire out and drive the defensive man back.
     B. One blocker pulls right and the other blocker blocks
        down.
     C. One blocker pulls left and the other blocker blocks
        down.

D. Both blockers use pass protection.

E. Both linemen pull in opposite directions.

Coaching points:

1. Defensive lineman explodes on movement and reacts to the blocking pattern.
2. Defensive man should go through the blocker, not around him.
3. Defensive man should get across the line and be ready to locate the ball and make the tackle.
4. Defensive man must protect his area first.

TYPE OF DRILL: Defensive reaction
NAME OF DRILL: 5-on-2
TO BE USED BY: Defensive Tackles
PURPOSE: To teach tackles to react to and play team-blocking schemes
SET UP:

1. Set up a five-man offensive front—center, two guards and two tackles.
2. Set up two defensive tackles in their normal alignment. The tackles may vary their alignment depending on the coach's philosophy of defense.

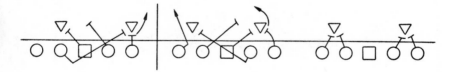

Diagram 5-12.

Instructions:

1. Coach calls a huddle and gives the offensive players their assignments and starting count.
2. The offense can run various patterns of blocking against the defensive tackles (Diagram 5-12).
3. The tackles fulfill their defensive obligations, protect their

area, control, disengage, locate ball and pursue or chase, depending on their defensive assignments.

4. Later on a backfield may be added to this drill to make it more realistic.

Coaching points:

1. The coach may want to set up a full defensive line and have everyone except the tackle hold dummies. In other words the only people that will be live are the tackles.
2. The coach obviously can do this for each position on the defensive line. It makes for great concentration in a particular area.

TYPE OF DRILL: Defensive shedding
NAME OF DRILL: Across-the-bow
TO BE USED BY: Defensive Linemen
PURPOSE: To teach defensive linemen to shed a blocker and react to the ball carrier.

SET UP:

1. Line up players on the sideline adjacent to a yard stripe.
2. Players pair off as they cross the sideline.
3. Designate one pair as blockers and the other as defensive men (Diagram 5-13).

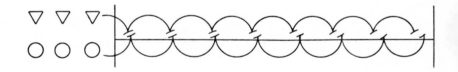

Diagram 5-13.

Instructions:

1. The players proceed across the width of the field in pairs.
2. The blocker uses a shoulder block, trying to keep the defensive man away from the imaginary ball carrier. The blocker tries to get his head and shoulders in front of the defensive man.

3. The defensive man moves laterally, using a forearm shiver, trying to keep the blocker from "getting his pads to him."

4. Each player, the blocker and the defensive man, stay on their side of the yard line.

5. The defensive man must be in a good football position with his head up, "eyeing" the ball carrier. He must not get tied up with the blocker.

6. Once the players reach the opposite side line, they come back across the field, this time the blocker becomes the defensive man and the defensive man the blocker.

Coaching points:

1. It is best to "walk and talk" this drill before going all out.

TYPE OF DRILL: Defensive reaction
NAME OF DRILL: Hit-shed-pursue-and-tackle
TO BE USED BY: Defensive Linemen
PURPOSE: To teach linemen to protect their area and to be ready to help in another area

SET UP:

1. Place four dummies on their side, two yards apart.
2. Place an offensive and defensive man in each hole.
3. Place a ball carrier outside the first dummy.

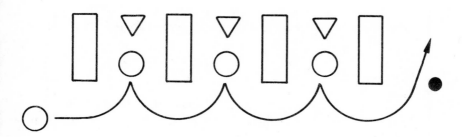

Diagram 5-14.

Instructions:

1. On the coach's signal, the offensive men fire out and protect their area.

2. The defensive men will move on movement of the offensive blocker's hand. They will hit, shed the blocker, and pursue the ball carrier.
3. The ball carrier will run through any hole that he sees open. If all holes are closed he will turn up field at the end of the fourth dummy (Diagram 5-14).
4. The movement of the defensive man, after the first hit, must be laterally, keeping his shoulder parallel to the line of scrimmage and keeping good position on the ball carrier.
5. Three defensive men should converge on the ball carrier at the point of contact.

Coaching points:

1. The coach should stress the point that a defensive lineman not only is responsible for his immediate area but that he must shed the blocker and locate the ball carrier.

TYPE OF DRILL: Defensive reaction
NAME OF DRILL: Shed-and-shuffle
TO BE USED BY: Defensive Linemen
PURPOSE: To teach a lineman to step, hit and shuffle—
                            step, hit and shuffle
SET UP:

1. Set up three dummies with holders in a diagonal line.
2. Set up lines of defensive men in front of the first dummy.
3. Set up two groups so that the players can react right and left.

Instructions:

1. The defensive player uses a forearm lift on the first dummy.
2. If the player is moving to his right he will use a left forearm lift to keep his head on the outside.
3. The defensive player proceeds in the same manner to the second and third dummies (Diagram 5-15).
4. The dummy simulates blockers coming at the defensive man who is trying to shed them and locate the ball carrier.
5. The defensive man should not get hung up on the dummy.

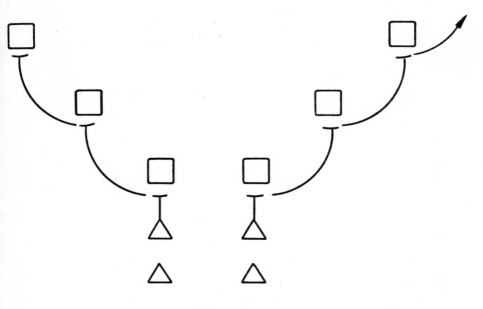

Diagram 5-15.

He must hit, come to a squared-up position and move to the next dummy.

6. The defensive man should always be in a good football-or-hit position with the feet chopping.

Coaching points:

1. The dummies should be light, or arm shield should be used, so that the blockers can move into the defensive man.
2. The defensive man holds the last dummy he hits and all holders move up and into line.

TYPE OF DRILL: Defensive
NAME OF DRILL: Pursuit-and-chase
TO BE USED BY: Defensive Linemen
PURPOSE: To teach a down defensive lineman when to chase and when to pursue while concentrating on proper angles

SET UP:

1. Set up four players with light dummies or arm shields.
2. Set up four players in front of the dummies in a four-point defensive stance.
3. Set up a ball carrier seven yards deep with a ball.
4. Set up two markers 20 yards apart to simulate boundaries for the ball carrier.

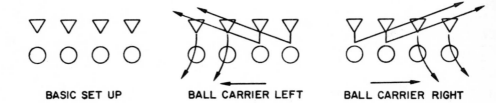

BASIC SET UP   **BALL CARRIER LEFT**   **BALL CARRIER RIGHT**

Diagram 5-16.

Instructions:

1. On the coach's command, or movement of the ball, the defensive man will: strike a blow; control the blocker; disengage the blocker; find the ball; pursue or chase; and simulate a form tackle on the ball carrier.
2. If the ball carrier runs left (defensive left) the two left defensive men will cross the line and *chase* the ball carrier. The two men on the right will *pursue* the ball carrier at a forty-five degree angle. The procedure is reversed if the ball carrier moves right (Diagram 5-16).

Coaching points:

1. Drill may be used live after techniques have been mastered.
2. Ball carrier may also show, pass, or run up the middle.
3. Drill may be used with ball carrier in the gap if this is the defense to be used.
4. All men should get to the ball carrier.
5. Offensive men become defensive men so that all get several chances at the drill.

TYPE OF DRILL: Defensive
NAME OF DRILL: Seat-roll-vs-the-sled
TO BE USED BY: Defensive Linemen
PURPOSE: To teach the seat roll, a defensive maneuver for linemen who have been hooked or knocked back by a blocker

SET UP:

1. Line up the players to the left of the seven-man charging sled.

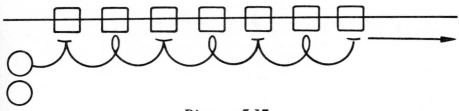

Diagram 5-17.

2. Players will proceed down the sled, attacking every other pad. When they hit the last pad, they will sprint 10 yards (Diagram 5-17).
3. After all players have gone from left to right, they will line up on the right of the sled and reverse the process.
4. Players should take two trips each way.

Instructions:

1. First player will line up in a four-point stance on the first pad.
2. The player strikes a blow with the right shoulder when going to his right.
3. The player then drops his hip in direction of the spin, rolls over on all fours, regroups and attacks the third pad, continues until he has hit every other pad, sprints 10 yards after hitting the last pad.

Coaching points:

1. The coach should make sure the "seat" never actually

touches the ground. When the player has his back to the ground, he is still on all fours.

TYPE OF DRILL: Defensive
NAME OF DRILL: Forearm-shiver-on-the-sled
TO BE USED BY: Defensive Linemen
PURPOSE: To teach and practice the forearm shiver on the seven-man sled
SET UP:

1. Line up the defensive players to the left of the sled.

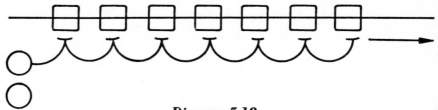

Diagram 5-18.

Instructions:

1. On the command of the coach, the first man in the line will move down the sled using a forearm shiver on each pad (Diagram 5-18). A T pad on the sled is excellent for this type of maneuver.
2. Once all players have progressed down the line, they will sprint 10 yards and then start back to the right. Always sprinting 10 yards after they hit the last dummy.

Coaching points:

1. The shiver is delivered with the palms and heels of the hands.
   The elbows are locked and the arms straight. The back is flat, knees flexed and head is up.
2. A short chopping movement of the feet should be encouraged and the feet should be kept away from the sled.
3. Two trips each way should be taken.
4. This drill also develops the arms and shoulders.

TYPE OF DRILL: Defensive
NAME OF DRILL: Forearm-lift-on-sled
TO BE USED BY: Defensive Linemen
PURPOSE: To teach and practice the forearm lift
SET UP:

1. Line up the defensive linemen to the left of the seven-man sled.

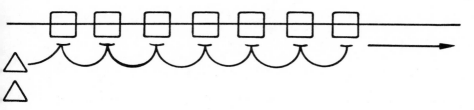

Diagram 5-19.

Instructions:

1. The first player in line will proceed down the sled, attacking each pad with a right forearm lift, regrouping after each hit (Diagram 5-19).
2. The next player in line will follow after the first player has progressed to the third or fourth pad.
3. Once all the players have gone through from the left side, they return using the same procedure only using their left forearm.
4. Usually two trips are taken each way.

Coaching points:

1. The forearm lift is delivered with the back of the hand, forearm, upper arm and shoulder. The main contact is made with the forearm, however.
2. The leg must work in conjunction with the lift, right arm, step with right foot, left arm, step with left foot.
3. This should be a short jab step.
4. Coach should emphasize a good blow and head up, in search of the ball carrier.

5. The "off" hand should be placed on the shoulder of the opponent.
6. After the last pad is hit, the player should sprint 10 yards to simulate closing in on the ball carrier.

TYPE OF DRILL: Defensive reaction
NAME OF DRILL: Spin-out vs the-seven-man sled
TO BE USED BY: Defensive Linemen
PURPOSE: To teach the spin-out, a defensive maneuver for defensive linemen who are "hooked" by a blocker
SET UP:

1. Line up the players to the left of the seven-man charging sled.
2. After the players have gone from left to right, they will line up to the right of the sled and reverse the process.

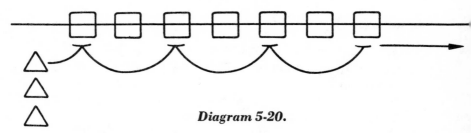

Diagram 5-20.

Instructions:

1. Players will proceed down the sled, attacking every other pad. When they hit the last pad they will sprint ten yards and get back in line (Diagram 5-20).
2. The player will strike a good blow on the first pad with a right shoulder block.
3. After the player has made contact he will spin-off the pad, keeping a tight arc.
4. On the spin, the player collapses his leg in the spin direction and drives off the other foot, pushing with his arms and hands.
5. When spinning right the player whips the left elbow in a natural plane for additional leverage and block breakdown.

Coaching points:

1. The coach should insist on a tight arc or good hit position to insure the closing of the blocking surface.
2. The coach should also insist that the player gather, and get in a good hit position for the next pad.

TYPE OF DRILL: Defensive reaction
NAME OF DRILL: Three-on-one
TO BE USED BY: Defensive Linemen
PURPOSE: To develop the defensive man's reaction to a straight-on block, a fill block or a double-team block

SET UP:

1. Three offensive men vs one defensive man.
2. Set up as many groups as feasible. The coach can move from one group to the next in rapid fire order.

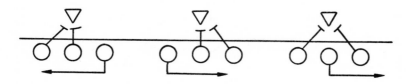

Diagram 5-21.

Instructions:

1. The coach will station himself behind the defensive man and indicate to the offensive men just what he wants them to do.
2. The coach will signal the starting count and the defensive man will move on first "movement" of the blocker's hand (Diagram 5-21).
3. The coach can move from one group to another and the defensive man rotates with the blockers. This should be done until all four of the people in the drill have had several shots at defense.

Coaching points:

1. The coach should teach the defensive man to always try and keep square with the line of scrimmage.
2. If there is a double-team, the defensive man should hold his ground and NOT try to go around the blockers.
3. Give the defensive man a plot of ground to protect and under no circumstance should he give this up.

TYPE OF DRILL: Fumble recovery
NAME OF DRILL: One-on-one-fumble-recovery
TO BE USED BY: All Linemen
PURPOSE: To practice recovering a fumble after disengaging a blocker

SET UP:

1. Set up one offensive blocker and one defensive man.
2. Coach stands three yards behind the blocker.

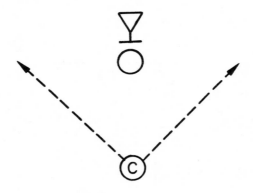

Diagram 5-22.

Instructions:

1. The defensive man works on a "one-on-one" situation with a blocker.
2. The defensive man hits, controls, disengages his blocker and protects his area (Diagram 5-22).
3. Mid-way through the one-on-one, the coach throws the ball on the ground, either right or left.

4. The defensive man must get "rid" of the blocker and re-cover the fumble.

Coaching points:

1. The coach will not throw the ball every time.
2. The defensive man must do "first things first" and that is to control the offensive blocker and protect his area.
3. He should not be conscious of the fumble until he sees the ball on the ground.

TYPE OF DRILL: Defensive reaction
NAME OF DRILL: Hit-and-pursue vs the sled
TO BE USED BY: Defensive Linemen
PURPOSE: To develop a good initial hit and proper pur-suit of the ball carrier

SET UP:

1. Set up linemen in three lines in front of the seven-man sled.
2. Players line up in front of the first, third, and fifth pads in a three or four-point stance.
3. Coach stations himself behind the sled.

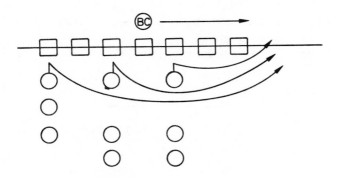

Diagram 5-23.

Instructions:

1. On movement of the coach, the players will fire out at the

sled and pursue in the direction as designated by the coach
(Diagram 5-23).
2. Three techniques may be used in contacting the sled:
   A. Shoulder charge.
   B. Forearm-shoulder charge.
   C. Forearm shiver.
3. A ball carrier may be stationed behind the sled and move
   left or right and the defensive players will react to his movement and form-tackle the ball carrier.

Coaching points:

1. The coach should stress the initial hit first before pursuing.
   The idea being that the defensive man has controlled the
   blocker and is now in position to pursue.

TYPE OF DRILL: Defensive reaction
NAME OF DRILL: Hit-pivot-and-pursue
TO BE USED BY: Defensive Linemen
PURPOSE: To develop a good initial charge, control,
                          balance and good pursuit angle
SET UP:

1. Set up linemen in three lines in front of the seven-man sled.
2. Players line up in front of the first, third and fifth pads in a
   three- or four-point stance.
3. Coach stations himself behind the sled.

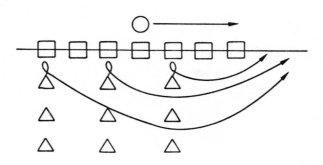

Diagram 5-24.

Instructions:

1. On movement of the coach, the players will fire out at the sled, pivot and pursue in the direction as designated by the coach (Diagram 5-24).
2. Three various techniques may be used in contacting the sled:
   A. Shoulder charge.
   B. Forearm/shoulder lift.
   C. Forearm shiver.
3. A ball carrier may be stationed behind the sled and move left or right and the defensive players will react to this movement and form tackle the ball carrier.

Coaching points:

1. The coach should stress the hit first and then the pivot and pursuit.
2. This maneuver is designed to teach a defensive man how to get away from a blocker who has him "hooked."

TYPE OF DRILL: Defensive reaction
NAME OF DRILL: Whirl-out vs the Sled
TO BE USED BY: Defensive Linemen
PURPOSE: Develops agility, balance, coordination and second effort. Also improves team pursuit.
SET UP:

1. Players from a single line on the end pad of the seven-man charging sled.

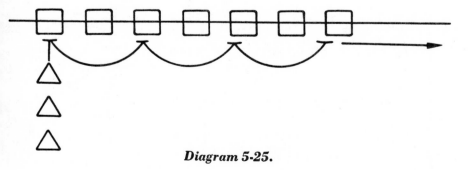

Diagram 5-25.

Instructions:

1. Players deliver a blow to the first pad, then whirl out, touching the hands to the ground.
2. The player then hits the third, whirls out touching hands to the ground (Diagram 5-25).
3. The players continue until they have hit the fifth and seventh pads and then they sprint ten yards toward the sideline.
4. The next man repeats the process. Once all men have completed the maneuver, they line up at the other end of the sled and start back down the sled.

Coaching points:

1. The main difference between the whirl-out and the spin-out is the touching of the hands to the ground between hits.
2. The touching of the hands to the ground teaches recovery and balance.

TYPE OF DRILL: Defensive hitting technique
NAME OF DRILL: Ten-twenty
TO BE USED BY: Defensive Linemen
PURPOSE: To teach defensive linemen how to strike a blow with the forearm/shoulder lift—becoming proficient with both the left and right arms
SET UP:

1. Set up two lines facing the two-man charging sled.
2. Set up two men with light dummies, one to the side of each pad

Instructions:

1. The coach, who is stationed on the sled, moves the pads and the defensive men strike the sled with a forearm/shoulder lift (Diagram 5-26).
2. If the player is right-handed he strikes the pad ten times with his right arm, and twenty times with his left arm.
3. The player hits, steps, regroups, hits, steps, regroups until he has done it ten or twenty times.

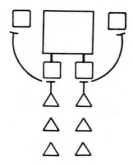

Diagram 5-26.

4. After the last hit he will shuffle out and use a form tackle on the dummy outside the sled. He then becomes the dummy holder.

Coaching points:

1. The purpose of this drill is to make a well-balance ball player, that is one who can use his left or right side equally.
2. Another gimmick for teaching this maneuver is to have the players try and tip the sled over. This is done without the coach standing on the sled.

TYPE OF DRILL: Defensive reaction
NAME OF DRILL: Shed-the-blocker-and-pursue vs the Sled
TO BE USED BY: Defensive Linemen
PURPOSE: To develop the ability to hit, come under control and hit again before pursuing
SET UP:

1. Set up linemen in three lines in front of the seven-man sled.
2. Players line up in front of the first, third and fifth pads in a three or four-point stance.
3. Coach stations himself behind the sled.

Instructions:

1. On movement of the coach, the players will fire out at the sled and pursue in the direction of their movement, that is,

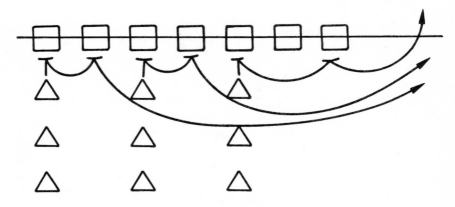

Diagram 5-27.

if they are moving right they will pursue right. The process is reversed when going left (Diagram 5-27).

2. Three various techniques may be used in contacting the sled:
   A. Shoulder charge.
   B. Forearm/shoulder lift.
   C. Forearm shiver.

3. After initial contact, the players drop off, regroup with feet chopping and hit the next pad.

4. After the last hit they will pursue laterally and sprint for ten yards.

Coaching points:

1. Proper form and a good football position or hitting position is desired at all times.

TYPE OF DRILL: Defensive reaction
NAME OF DRILL: Hit-pivot-and-shed vs the Sled
TO BE USED BY: Defensive Linemen
PURPOSE: To develop the ability to pivot out of a block and shed the second blocker before pursuing down the line

SET UP:

1. Set up linemen in three lines in front of the seven-man sled.

2. Players line up in front of the first, third and fifth pads in a three or four-point stance.
3. Coach stations himself behind the sled.

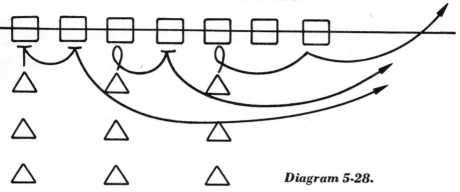

Diagram 5-28.

Instructions:

1. On movement of the coach, the players will fire out at the sled and pivot to the next pad.
2. After hitting the second pad, the players again pivot and pursue the ball carrier (Diagram 5-28).
3. Three various techniques may be used in contacting the sled:
   A. Shoulder charge.
   B. Forearm/shoulder lift.
   C. Forearm shiver.
4. After all players have progressed through the sled to the right, they will reverse the process and come back to the left.

Coaching points:

1. This drill is designed to teach a player who has been "hooked" by a blocker, to pivot out and be ready for the next blocker.
2. The drill also teaches balance, coordination and agility.

TYPE OF DRILL: Defensive fundamentals
NAME OF DRILL: Block-Protection
TO BE USED BY: Defensive Linemen

PURPOSE: To teach and develop several methods for
                          protecting the defensive man from the offen-
                          sive blocker

SET UP:

1. Players pair off. Designate one as offense and one as defense
   (Diagram 5-29).
2. Coach will huddle the defensive player and designate the
   type of technique to be used.
3. The coach should work one group at a time until all the
   skills have been mastered. The coach may then work a two-
   on-two, three-on-three or any size group that is feasible.

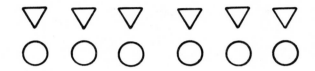

Diagram 5-29.

Instructions:

1. The offensive blocker will fire out in an effort to control the
   defensive man.
2. The defensive man will pursue one of the following techniques as called by the coach:
   A. Low Shoulder and Forearm Charge
      a. Step with the back foot, keeping body low, and drive
         shoulder into the blocker neutralizing his charge.
         The defensive man should try to step on the blocker's
         toes in order to keep his legs under him.
      b. The defensive player should drive his corresponding
         forearm up under the blocker's chest, trying to lift
         him.
      c. The heel of the free hand should be driven into the
         opponent's shoulder pads for further control.
      d. The defensive man should then locate the ball, shed
         opponent and pursue or chase.
   B. Rip Up and Lift
      a. On movement of the blocker, the defensive man

steps with his back foot to a squared-up position.

b. Using the corresponding arm to the rear foot, the defensive man drives his forearm across the opponent's chest and tries to lift his opponent.

c. The heel of the free hand should be driven into the opponent's shoulder pads.

d. The defensive man should locate the ball, shed the opponent and pursue or chase the ball carrier.

e. The only difference between the "rip and lift" and "shoulder and lift" is the use of the shoulder block in the initial charge. The shoulder charge must be used vs a bigger and stronger opponent.

C. Hand Shiver

a. On movement of the blocker, the defensive man steps with his back foot to a squared-up position and drives the heels of the hands up and under the blocker's shoulder pads, keeping his elbows locked.

b. Constant pressure must be maintained by use of the hands while moving the feet in a chopping motion.

c. The defensive man should locate the ball, shed the opponent and pursue or chase the ball carrier.

d. The object of the forearm shiver is to keep the blocker away from the defensive man's body.

D. Slant Charge

a. On movement of the offensive blocker, the defensive man slants right or left, depending on the call.

b. The defensive man crosses over with the foot away from the slant, and uses his inside hand to keep the blocker away from his knees.

c. The defensive man should not hesitate and should explode right or left. The defensive man can either line up on the line of scrimmage or off the line depending on the technique the coach desires.

d. If slanting into another man on the line, the defensive man should drive into him with a hand shiver and keep going in that direction.

e. If the defensive man feels pressure from the blocker in front of him, he should drive into him using the inside hand as leverage and pursue around his pressure.

E. Loop Charge

    a. Defensive man lines up off the line of scrimmage.

    b. Step with the near foot in the direction of the loop, cross over step with the far foot and pivot into the man who is one man down the line.

    c. Use a hand shiver on the next man, control him, locate ball, shed him and pursue or chase.

    d. The defensive man must move quickly and should never get caught halfway through his move.

F. Dip Charge

    a. This maneuver should be used when playing in the gap.

    b. On movement of the ball or nearest opponent, the defensive man drops the outside shoulder and knee, and penetrates one yard deep into the backfield.

    c. The defensive man should come under control with a lifting motion and play football from there. Grab all legs in your area.

TYPE OF DRILL: Defensive reaction

NAME OF DRILL: Reacting-to-the-Sweeps or Pass

TO BE USED BY: Defensive Linemen

PURPOSE: To teach the down linemen the proper angles of pursuing or chasing and how to react to a pass

SET UP:

1. Set up four linemen facing the coach.
2. Set up three men who will catch the ball for the coach. One on either side of the four men and one behind them.

Instructions:

1. This drill is designed to teach the defensive lineman how to react for the sweeps and the pass, and is a warm-up drill for the pursue and chase drill.
2. The coach stations himself five yards in front of the defensive men with a ball.

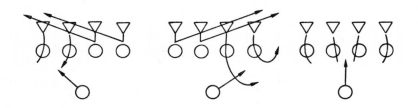

Diagram 5-30.

3. When the coach moves the ball, the defensive men make their initial movement as to strike a blow on the opponent.
4. The coach then throws the ball right, left or down the middle. If the ball is thrown right, the two left defensive men chase the ball and the two on the far side pursue the ball. If the ball is thrown left the procedure is reversed (Diagram 5-35).
5. If the ball is thrown down the middle the players react to pass.

Coaching points:

1. The coach should use the pursue and chase drill next, and the pass-rush wall drill following. Each drill complements one another.

TYPE OF DRILL: Defensive control
NAME OF DRILL: Board
TO BE USED BY: Defensive Linemen
PURPOSE: To teach a defensive lineman to neutralize, control and disengage his opponent
SET UP:

1. Players pair off, designate one as a blocker and one as a defensive man.
2. Set up the defensive player, straddling a board (2″ × 12″ × 8′ long).
3. Set up the offensive player facing the defensive player (Diagram 5-31). Actually this is one-on-one on the board.
4. Set up as many groups as feasible.

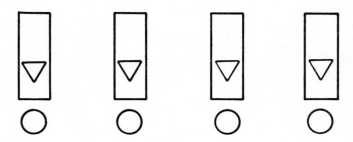

Diagram 5-31.

Instructions:

1. The coach may work all groups together or rotate from one group to another.
2. The coach will give the blocker the starting count, and on first movement the defensive man will strike a blow.
3. The object of the drill is for the blocker to drive the defensive man off the board.
4. The object of the defensive man is to strike a blow, neutralize the opponent's charge, disengage the opponent and control his area.
5. To be effective in this drill the defensive man should end up in his original position, that is, he still should be straddling the board in a low football position and the blocker should be thrown off the board.

Coaching points:

1. This drill may be started with the defensive man holding a dummy while the blocker tries to push him back.

TYPE OF DRILL: Defensive—Rushing the passer
NAME OF DRILL: Get-to-them
TO BE USED BY: Defensive Linemen
PURPOSE: To provide practice for the interior line in the pass rush
SET UP:

1. Set up two lines of four, one representing the offensive line and one the defensive line.

2. Have the offensive people hold light dummies or wear arm shields.
3. Set up a standing dummy, representing the passer, about 7 yards deep (Diagram 5-32).

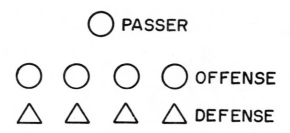

Diagram 5-32.

Instructions:

1. On the coach's command, the defensive linemen will try to get to the passer (dummy) as fast as they can.
2. The offensive linemen using pass protection techniques, will try to keep the defensive linemen away from the dummy.
3. The coach should put a stop-watch on this drill and all the defensive linemen should have reached the dummy by a certain time. Usually five seconds would be the maximum time.

Coaching points:

1. This drill may be used live.
2. It becomes a real competitive drill.
3. The defensive man should never give up until he has reached the dummy.
4. Every once in a while take the stop watch off and let the troops go until everyone has reached the dummy. Very interesting!!

TYPE OF DRILL: Defensive—Pass rush
NAME OF DRILL: Hit-and-rush vs the Sled
TO BE USED BY: Defensive Linemen

PURPOSE: To teach how to neutralize the blocker, dis-
                    engage and rush the passer

SET UP:

1. Set up two lines in front of the two-man sled.
2. Station two "quarterbacks" to the rear of the sled.
3. Station the coach on the sled.

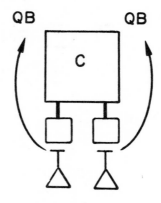

QB   **QB**

Diagram 5-33.

Instructions:

1. On movement by the coach, the defensive man delivers a
   blow to the pads on the sled.
2. The defensive man releases quickly and rushes the quarterback who will simulate drop back action (Diagram 5-33).
3. After rushing the passer, the rusher becomes the quarterback.

Coaching points:

1. The rusher uses short choppy steps and places his hands on
   the quarterback's shoulders.
2. The rusher should contain the quarterback and have balance enough to move right or left.

TYPE OF DRILL: Defensive-pass rush
NAME OF DRILL: Pass-rush vs 2-man Sled vs Sprint and Roll-
                 out Passer

TO BE USED BY: Defensive Linemen

PURPOSE: To strike a blow, read pass and rush the passer

SET UP:

1. Set up two defensive men in front of the 2-man sled.
2. Set up two dummies with holders on each side of the sled.
3. Set up one quarterback behind the sled.

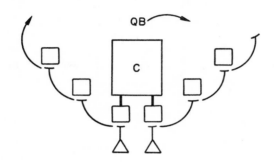

Diagram 5-34.

Instructions:

1. On the signal, the quarterback will sprint or roll right or left.
2. The defensive men, on movement of the quarterback will react to the pass.
3. They will strike a blow on the sled pad, work through the two dummies and get to the passer (Diagram 5-34).
4. The defensive man may use any type of charge, forearm lift, shoulder, shiver, spin-out or seat-roll.
5. When they get to the passer they will form tackle.
6. The backside rusher will contain and chase from the backside.
7. The quarterback can "roll" back to the other side on occasions just to keep the back side man honest.

Coaching points:

1. The coach should stress outside contain.
2. The coach may use his own innovations on this drill. He

may want to use live blockers instead of dummies. He may want to have the quarterback carry a light dummy so that the form tackle can be more effective.

TYPE OF DRILL: Defensive—Pass rush recognition
NAME OF DRILL: Buckley-wall
TO BE USED BY: Defensive Linemen
PURPOSE: To teach defensive linemen to react to an intercepted or completed pass after they have rushed the passer

SET UP:

1. Set up four defensive linemen in a down position.
2. Set up a center, passer and a simulated end, two yards downfield.

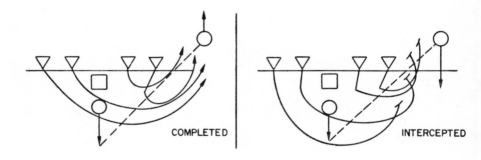

Diagram 5-35.   **Diagram 5-36.**

Instructions:

1. On the snap, the linemen rush the passer. When they get one yard from the passer, they come to a set position with their hands up and yell "pass." The passer throws right or left.
2. If the passer throws the ball to the right, the defenders take off in that direction, if he throws to the left they move in that direction.
3. If the end takes off up-field, the linemen chase him simulating a completed pass (Diagram 5-35).

4. If the end yells "bingo," comes back toward the passer, simulating an intercepted pass, the linemen form a picket wall, picking up any opponent who attempts to tackle the intercepter (Diagram 5-36).

Coaching points:

1. This is a must drill at the completion of any pass protection or pass-rush drill.
2. The coach should stress good balance and body control when rushing the passer.

TYPE OF DRILL: Defensive pass rush
NAME OF DRILL: Mazzucca-speed
TO BE USED BY: Defensive Linemen
PURPOSE: To develop speed in getting off the hook and
                                  to the passer
SET UP:

1. Line two yard area with dummies or cones.
2. Set up a blocker and a rusher at one end of the lane.
3. Set up simulated quarterback with a light dummy at the other end of the lane, five to seven yards deep.

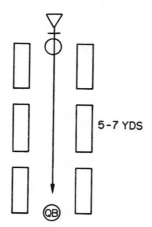

Diagram 5-37.

Instructions:

1. Blocker will try to keep pass rusher out of the lane (Diagram 5-37).
2. Rusher will try to get rid of the blocker as fast as possible.
3. Once the rusher has "cleared" the blocker he will take a straight path to the quarterback and make a form tackle.
4. Coach should put a stop-watch on this drill.

Coaching points:

1. Pass rusher should maintain a straight line to the quarterback and come under balance and control when making contact. He should make a high tackle to simulate going after the ball.

CHAPTER SIX

Winning Drills for the Tackling Linemen

"EIGHTY PERCENT HEART—TWENTY PERCENT SKILL"

The eighty percent heart we can't do much about so we have to confine our teaching ability and techniques to the twenty percent skill.

There are many ways to teach tackling and there are many mechanical devices that are available, but the most important thing in teaching tackling is to build self-confidence in the players. This can only be done by properly teaching the fundamentals of tackling.

One of the most important factors in teaching tackling is that in the early stages of tackling, the players should be paired off as equally as possible in regards to size. This is not always possible but in the lower levels of football this can be done without much trouble.

Most of the drills listed on the next few pages are basic fundamental drills. When you break down the techniques of tackling you realize that there are only three ways a runner may be tackled: head on, from the side, and from the rear.

Some basic factors in tackling should be followed:

1. To be a good tackler one must be keyed up emotionally. Aggressiveness and determination are essential.
2. The preliminary position for tackling should always put a tackler in a ready position to make the tackle: good base, bull neck with head and shoulders up, butt low, legs bent at a 45-degree angle, eyes open and feet chopping.
3. The tackle is nothing more than a shoulder block after which the arms are wrapped around the ball carrier.
4. The tackler should always tackle through the runner.
5. A good axiom for tackling is: I must make the tackle or it will be a touchdown.

Players should be keyed emotionally before tackling begins, the coach plays an important part in the spirit of the drill. Once the player gains self-confidence in tackling, the eighty percent heart takes over. Tackling is probably one of the most natural things we do in football, as kids we played tag, we wrestled, it is all relative.

On the other hand, in today's technological society we do not go around tackling people every day, hence the drills should lead us back to one of our natural instincts.

Players should learn the fundamentals on the blocking dummies, charging sleds, hanging dummies before they tackle live.

TYPE OF DRILL: Beginning tackling
NAME OF DRILL: Walk-Through Tackling
TO BE USED BY: Defensive Linemen
PURPOSE: To teach the proper fundamentals of tackling

SET UP:

1. Players pair off. Set up as many lines as feasible.
2. Start the drill with the players about two yards apart (Diagram 6-1).

Instructions:

1. Designate one line as ball carriers and one line as tacklers.
2. The tacklers will walk up to the ball carriers and assume a football position.

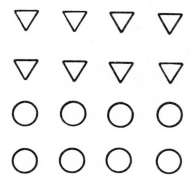

Diagram 6-1.

3. The tackler will use a left or right shoulder, depending on the call of the coach. The tackler should place his head on the ball carrier's numbers before sliding to one shoulder or the other.
4. The tackler wraps his arms around the ball carrier's knees, grabbing his wrists behind the ball carrier at the same time pulling his knees together.
5. At the moment of impact the ball carrier assists by "folding" over the tackler's shoulder.
6. The tackler picks up the ball carrier and walks a few steps.
7. The tackler should: keep his head up (bull neck), eyes open, back straight and feet apart.

Coaching points:

1. The coach should stress the Hit-and-Lift action.
2. The coach may pick up the momentum in this drill as the fundamentals are learned.
3. Players should pair off according to size.

TYPE OF DRILL: Tackling
NAME OF DRILL: Confidence Tackling
TO BE USED BY: Defensive Linemen
PURPOSE: To teach players how to tackle and practice before they have live contact—also to build confidence in tackling

SET UP:

1. Players pair off, one as a dummy holder and one as a tackler.
2. Start the drill with the tackler one yard from the dummy. The drill may progress until the tackler is five yards away from the dummy (Diagram 6-2).
3. Set up as many groups as feasible.

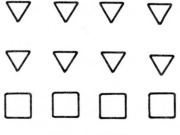

Diagram 6-2.

Instructions:

1. The tacklers make contact with the dummy with either the right or left shoulder, depending on the call of the coach.
2. The player hits the bags just as if he was going to make a shoulder block, and then he whips his arms around the dummy and grabs his wrists in the back.
3. The player then drives through the dummy.
4. The players should keep their head up, bull neck, feet apart, back straight, eyes open and their arms should "whip" around the dummy.

Coaching points:

1. After a few hits the tacklers can move back to a maximum of five yards.
2. This drill may also be accomplished on a charging sled or a swinging dummy.
3. The coach should be more interested in tackling form rather than the hit.

TYPE OF DRILL: Tackling

NAME OF DRILL: Rhythm-reaction and Tackle
TO BE USED BY: Defensive Linemen
PURPOSE: To learn how to strike a blow and react to the ball carrier
SET UP:

1. Set up two offensive men, one defensive man and a ball carrier.
2. Set up as many groups as feasible.

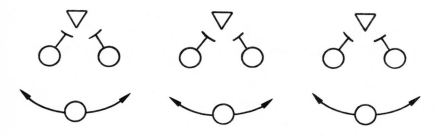

Diagram 6-3.

Instructions:

1. On the signal of the coach, the defensive man will react to the blocker on the right. He will get back in his original position and react to the blocker on the left (Eagle drill—Diagram 6-3).
2. Each time the defensive man reacts, the coach will say "HIT," after several hits by each blocker, the coach will say "go" and the ball carrier will run right or left.
3. The defensive man will then pursue or chase the ball carrier.

Coaching points:

1. The defensive man should be concerned with the blocker first and the ball carrier second.
2. The coach will set the rhythm for this drill and have the defensive man react to the ball carrier when he least expects it.
3. The blockers take only one shot at the defensive man and then get back in their stance.

4. This drill resembles the Eagle drill, with the exception that a ball carrier is added.

TYPE OF DRILL: Reaction and tackling
NAME OF DRILL: Through-a-man
TO BE USED BY: Defensive Linemen
PURPOSE: To teach a down lineman to hit, neutralize, disengage a blocker and to tackle the ball carrier

SET UP:

1. Set up a defensive man, a blocker and a ball carrier.
2. Place markers three yards apart to simulate the area which the defensive man must protect (Diagram 6-4).
3. Set up as many groups as feasible.

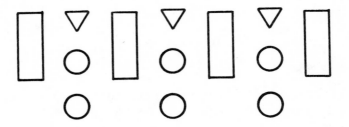

Diagram 6-4.

Instructions:

1. On the signal from the coach, the blocker will try to clear the area for the ball carrier.
2. The ball carrier will run inside the markers to the side of the blocker's head.
3. The defensive man will make contact, neutralize the block, disengage the blocker and make the tackle.
4. The tackle should be made as close to the line of scrimmage as possible. That is, the defensive man should not be driven back.
5. After the completion of the drill, the ball carrier becomes the defensive man, the defensive man the blocker and the blocker the ball carrier.

Coaching points:

1. This drill may be used as an offensive blocking drill, but in the case of above, the coach should stress the play of the defensive man.
2. This drill may also be used for linebackers. Place the linebacker off the ball about two yards and have him react to the blocker and make the tackle.

TYPE OF DRILL: Tackling
NAME OF DRILL: Angle-tackling
TO BE USED BY: Defensive Linemen
PURPOSE: To practice tackling from the side
SET UP:

1. Divide the players in four groups, two lines of ball carriers and two lines of tacklers.
2. Start the lines ten yards apart.
3. Place a marker five yards away from the first man in line on a 45-degree angle.
4. The coach stands in the middle of the two groups.

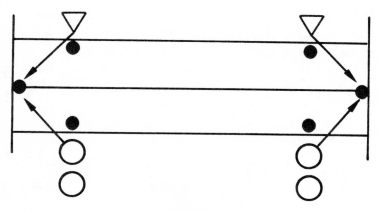

Diagram 6-5.

Instructions:

1. The coach works one group at a time.
2. On the signal from the coach, the ball carriers start for the marker (Diagram 6-5).

3. The tackler tries to make the tackle before the ball carrier reaches the marker.
4. Upon contact, the tackler should wrap his arms around the ball carrier's mid-section, place his shoulder pad on the ball carrier's hip pad and with the aid of his head turn the ball carrier back.

Coaching points:

1. This drill should be started at a slow pace with the lines only five yards apart. Stress proper form.
2. Players alternate lines so that the ball carriers become the tacklers and the tacklers the ball carriers. Also, they should alternate right and left.

TYPE OF DRILL: Tackling
NAME OF DRILL: Roll-and-tackle
TO BE USED BY: Defensive Linemen
PURPOSE: To teach proper form tackling and to develop increased agility by players reacting off the ground

SET UP:

1. Players pair off with partners of equal size, five yards apart.
2. Ball carriers have their backs to the tacklers.
3. Tacklers recline on their back, head pointed towards ball carrier.

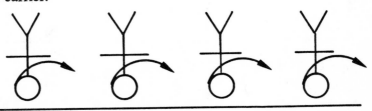

Diagram 6-6.

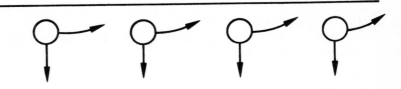

Instructions:

1. Coach will tell the ball carriers which way to run.
2. On the signal from the coach, the ball carriers turn and run at ¾ speed in the indicated direction (Diagram 6-6).
3. Tacklers whip over, recover to their feet and execute a form-tackle.
4. Tacklers should drive up through the ball carrier, lifting him off the ground.

Coaching points:

1. Coach should stress quick recovery from the ground.
2. Coach should explain that he never wants his players on their backs and that this is just done for drill purposes.

TYPE OF DRILL: Tackling
NAME OF DRILL: Explosive Form Tackling
TO BE USED BY: Defensive Linemen
PURPOSE: To teach players to explode through the numbers of a ball carrier from a hitting position

SET UP:

1. Set up two lines of tacklers.
2. Have one man, designated as the ball carrier, line up facing the two lines (Diagram 6-7).
3. Players alternate lines after performing the drill.

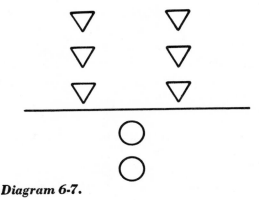

Diagram 6-7.

Instructions:

1. Ball carrier runs forward in an upright position.
2. The tacklers explode, driving their inside shoulders up and through the ball carrier's numbers.
3. The tacklers try to knock the ball carrier down with one blow and then recover.
4. The ball carrier runs forward two or three times, then a new player moves up.
5. The drill may be started with the ball carriers using a light dummy.

Coaching points:

1. Tacklers must anchor their outside foot and can only move their inside foot when exploding.
2. Tacklers should drive through the ball carrier, stressing the power that comes from the thighs and buttocks.
3. Tacklers must return to proper hitting position after each hit.

TYPE OF DRILL: Tackling
NAME OF DRILL: Sideline Tackling
TO BE USED BY: Defensive Linemen
PURPOSE: To teach players to react to ball carrier's open field moves and to get in good position to make the tackle
SET UP:

1. Set up two standing dummies facing the sideline.
2. Place the dummies five yards from the sideline with a tackler between them.
3. Place the ball carrier five yards in front of the first dummy, facing the goal line.

Instructions:

1. The ball carrier will start upfield between the dummies, headed for the goal line.
2. The tackler, facing the sideline to simulate a pursuit angle, will attempt to make the tackle, or drive the ball carrier out of bounds (Diagram 6-8).

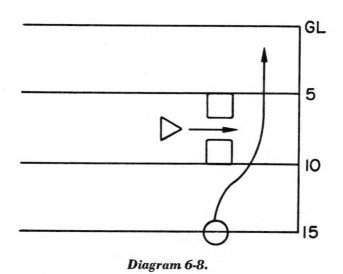

Diagram 6-8.

3. The tackler should not let the ball carrier cut back to the middle of the field.
4. The tackler should keep his head in front of the ball carrier and have his knees flexed, back straight and a bull neck.
5. The tackler should whip his arms around the ball carrier and never go to the ground.

Coaching points:

1. The coach may want to start this drill as a form tackling drill and have the ball carrier use a light dummy or shield.

TYPE OF DRILL: Tackling
NAME OF DRILL: Abe Martin
TO BE USED BY: Defensive Linemen
PURPOSE: To teach a defensive player to react to pressure, "get off the hook" and make the tackle
SET UP:

1. Set up two offensive linemen and one defensive lineman.
2. Set up as many groups as feasible.
3. Set up two markers as boundaries.
4. The coach stands behind the defensive men.

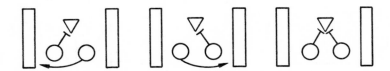

Diagram 6-9.

Instructions:

1. The coach will tell the offensive men what to do by use of hand signals.
2. The offensive men work in various combinations. That is, one man will pull and the other man will fill or any such offensive maneuver.
3. The defensive man reacts to the pressure of the man that is filling, gets off the hook and tries to tackle the pulling man (Diagram 6-9).
4. If the defensive man can beat the fill-in man, he then chases the pulling lineman.
5. If the defensive man cannot beat the fill-in man he either goes through the head of the blocker or does a spin-out and pursues the pulling man.

Coaching points:

1. Players rotate so that they all have a chance to become the defensive man.

TYPE OF DRILL: Tackling
NAME OF DRILL: Triangle
TO BE USED BY: Defensive Linemen
PURPOSE: To practice tackling form and reaction
SET UP:

1. Place three standing dummies in a triangle.
2. Set up one line of ball carriers and one line of tacklers.
3. Each line starts five yards from the center dummy.

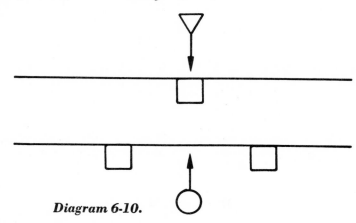

Diagram 6-10.

Instructions:

1. On the signal from the coach, the ball carrier heads for the center dummy and cuts right or left.
2. The tackler comes forward and tries to tackle the ball carrier before he passes through the triangle (Diagram 6-10).

Coaching points:

1. The coach stresses good tackling form, head up, bull neck, back straight and feet moving in a chopping motion.

TYPE OF DRILL: Tackling
NAME OF DRILL: Through-a-blocker
TO BE USED BY: Defensive Linemen
PURPOSE: To teach a defensive man to shed a moving blocker and get to the ball carrier and make the tackle

SET UP:

1. Set up a player with a light dummy or arm shields in front of a ball carrier.
2. Set up a defensive man in a two-point stance (football position) five yards away.
3. Set up markers five yards apart for a boundary for the ball carrier to move within.

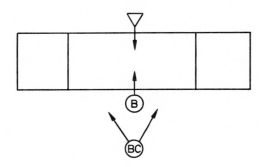

Diagram 6-11.

Instructions:

1. On the signal from the coach, both groups move forward.
2. The blocker, with the dummy, tries to keep the defensive man away from the ball carrier.
3. The ball carrier tries to stay behind his blocker and make it across the "line" (Diagram 6-11).
4. The tackler must shed the blocker and make the tackle.
5. This can either be a form-tackling drill or live. That is, the blocker will block live and not use the dummy or arm shields.

Coaching points:

1. The coach should insist on the tackler making contact on the line not five yards downfield. He should not give ground and should shed the blocker as rapidly as possible.

TYPE OF DRILL: Tackling
NAME OF DRILL: Form-explosion
TO BE USED BY: Defensive Linemen
PURPOSE: To practice straight ahead or head-on tackling, emphasizing the proper position of neck, back and legs while exploding into the ball carrier
SET UP:

1. Set up four lines, two tackling lines, and two lines of ball carriers.

2. The ball carriers will carry light air dummies or shields.
3. The coach will stand at the point of contact and will alternate lines, watching one and then the other.
4. The tackler should start five yards away from the ball carrier. Note: when first using this drill the ball carrier and tackler should only be two yards apart.

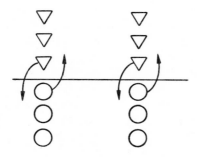

Diagram 6-12.

Instructions:

1. On the coach's signal, both men come forward.
2. The tackler will explode into the shield and try to knock the ball barrier back (Diagram 6-12).
3. The concentration should be on the proper "football position" of the tackler at the point of contact. The neck is bulled, the back straight, the knees bent at a 45-degree angle and the head up.

Coaching points:

1. The coach should not be too concerned with the arms on this drill as it is difficult to wrap the arms around the ball carrier while carrying a dummy. The concentration is on form and explosion.

TYPE OF DRILL: Tackling
NAME OF DRILL: Goal-line-tackling
TO BE USED BY: Defensive Linemen
PURPOSE: To teach the tackler to hit and drive the ball

carrier back instead of letting the ball carrier's momentum carry him over the goal
line

SET UP:

1. Set up two lines, one designated as ball carriers and one
   designated as tacklers.
2. Set up this drill on the five-yard line, five yards in from the
   sideline.
3. Use the sideline for one boundary and place a marker, five
   yards in, as the other boundary. In other words work in a
   five-yard square.

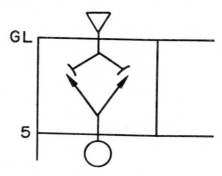

Diagram 6-13.

Instructions:

1. On the signal, the coach throws the ball to the ball carrier
   who tries to cross the goal line. He must stay within his
   square.
2. The tackler who starts on the goal line, tries to make contact as soon as possible and keep the ball carrier from
   scoring (Diagram 6-13).
3. Alternate lines after each drill.

Coaching points:

1. The coach must stress to the tackler that he must drive the
   ball carrier back and not let him score.
2. The coach may want to add a blocker to this drill after the
   skills have been mastered.

TYPE OF DRILL: Tackling
NAME OF DRILL: Oklahoma-tackling
TO BE USED BY: Defensive Linemen
PURPOSE: To teach linemen to react to a ball carrier after being knocked down
SET UP:

1. Pair off, have one man lying on his back with his head toward the ball carrier.
2. Have one man in an upright position, five yards away. This man, the ball carrier, faces away from the tackler and has a football on the ground in front of him.
3. Place markers about five yards apart to simulate the running lane.

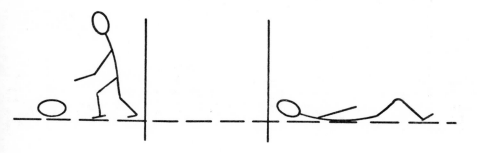

Diagram 6-14.

Instructions:

1. On the signal from the coach, the ball carrier picks up the ball, turns and runs between the boundaries (Diagram 6-14).
2. The tackler gets off the ground into a football position and makes the tackle.

Coaching points:

1. As an alternative, the coach may start both men on their backs. On the coach's signal, he will designate the tackler Both men spring to their feet and the tackler makes the tackle.

TYPE OF DRILL: Tackling
NAME OF DRILL: Cat-and-mouse
TO BE USED BY: Defensive Linemen
PURPOSE: To teach the tackler proper tackling form
                            and how to stay with the ball carrier
SET UP:

1. Set up two lines facing each other, designate one line as tacklers and one line as ball carriers.
2. Set up markers five yards apart on a yard-line to simulate the boundaries.
3. Set up two drills adjacent to each other so that the coach can watch one drill while the other group is getting ready. The coach alternates groups.
4. Players change lines after each drill.

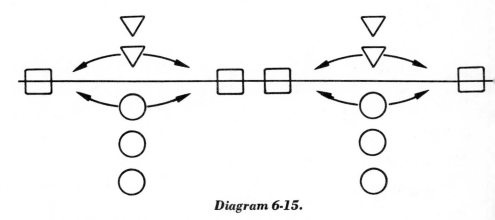

Diagram 6-15.

Instructions:

1. On the command "Move" the ball carrier will move back and forth on his side of the line.
2. The tackler will "mirror" the ball carrier, staying in front of him in a proper football position (Diagram 6-15).
3. On the command "Go," the ball carrier will try to cross the line and the tackler will tackle him.
4. The tackler tries to make the tackle before the ball carrier crosses the line. The line simulates the goal line and if the ball carrier crosses it it is a touchdown.

Coaching points:

1. The coach may say "Go" before he says "Move," just to keep the players alert.

TYPE OF DRILL: Tackling
NAME OF DRILL: Obstacle-tackling
TO BE USED BY: Defensive Linemen
PURPOSE: To develop recovery, body control and proper tackling form
SET UP:

1. Set up three dummies on the ground in a cross-wise fashion, two yards apart. Set up one dummy lengthwise, three or four yards in front of the other dummies.
2. Players line up in two lines facing each other at the end of the dummies.

Diagram 6-16.

Instructions:

1. The tackler assumes a four-point stance one yard from the lengthwise dummy.
2. On the command from the coach, the tackler drives the first dummy about three yards. The tackler then scrambles over the other dummies in a crab-like motion (Diagram 6-16).
3. He recovers off the ground and makes a form-tackle on the ball carrier, who starts forward when the tackler crosses the last dummy.
4. The next tackler pulls the first dummy back into position and assumes a four point stance.

Coaching points:

1. Tackler should keep his head up at all times.

2. Explosion, leg drive and quick recovery should be stressed.
3. Coach must time the drill so that the ball carrier does not start forward too soon.

TYPE OF DRILL: Tackling
NAME OF DRILL: Tackling vs the Two-Man Sled
TO BE USED BY: Defensive Linemen
PURPOSE: To stress good form and explosion in tack-ling

SET UP:

1. Set up one line facing the sled with the first man five yards from the sled.

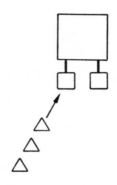

Diagram 6-17.

Instructions:

1. One man tackles the sled at a time.
2. No one stands on the sled because the purpose of the drill is to Hit, Lift and Drive.
3. The tackler approaches the sled from the outside with his head up and feet moving in a chopping motion. He clamps his arms around the pads, lifts and drives (Diagram 6-17).
4. Once the skill of hitting the sled has been mastered, the coach may want two tacklers to the sled at the same time.

Coaching points:

1. The tackler should really unload into the sled, stress the

fact that it is nothing more than a shoulder block with the arms whipped around the pad.

TYPE OF DRILL: Tackling
NAME OF DRILL: Hit-shuffle-and-tackle vs the Sled
TO BE USED BY: Defensive Linemen
PURPOSE: To develop skill in adjusting quickly from one alignment to another
SET UP:

1. Players form three lines in front of the seven-man charging sled.
2. First player in each line assumes a four-point stance one yard in front of the pad.

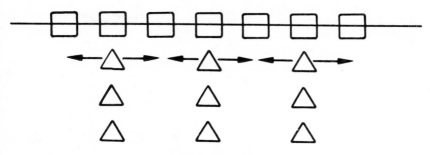

Diagram 6-18.

Instructions:

1. On the command of the coach, players deliver a blow to the sled.
2. Player recovers and moves on all fours to the next pad (left or right as designated from the coach).
3. Coach gives signal and player hits pad with opposite shoulder and forearm (Diagram 6-18).
4. Player recovers and moves back to the original pad.
5. Coach gives signal and player tackles the original pad.

Coaching points:

1. Players should not raise up when moving from one pad to the next.

2. Coach keeps players moving using the command, Hit, Hit, Tackle.
3. Players should always be in proper position when hitting the pads.

TYPE OF DRILL: Tackling
NAME OF DRILL: Form-tackling vs the Sled
TO BE USED BY: Defensive Linemen
PURPOSE: To develop proper form in tackling
SET UP:

1. Form lines of three in front of the seven-man sled (Diagram 6-19).

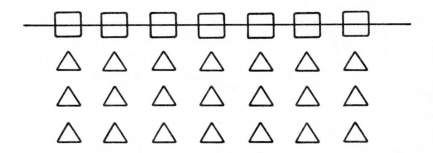

Diagram 6-19.

Instructions:

1. The first man in each line assumes a four-point stance in front of each pad.
2. On the signal from the coach, the player drives forward, explodes into the pad, wraps his arms around the pad and tries to lift.
3. The front of the sled should be raised off the ground at point of contact and should be maintained in the air until players stop driving their feet.
4. Players keep driving until coach blows his whistle.

Coaching points:

1. Players must keep back arched, feet shoulder-width apart in a chopping motion.

2. Players should not over-extend.
3. Players should hit up and through the sled.

TYPE OF DRILL: Tackling
NAME OF DRILL: Seat-roll-and-tackle vs the Sled
TO BE USED BY: Defensive Linemen
PURPOSE: To develop explosion while delivering a blow and quickness, agility and body control in locating the ball carrier.
SET UP:

1. Set up one line in front of the two man charging sled.
2. Coach stations himself on the sled.

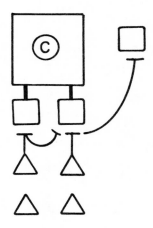

Diagram 6-20.

Instructions:

1. First player in the line assumes a four-point stance in front of the sled.
2. On movement of the coach, the defensive man delivers a blow to the pad.
3. The player then does a seat-roll and recovers and tackles the next pad.
4. The next man in line assumes a four-point stance and hits the pad as soon as the man in front of him has made the tackle (Diagram 6-20).

5. The coach should stress "rolling across the fanny" and re-covering quickly off of the ground.

Coaching points:

1. The coach should stress proper tackling form and the head should be outside of the pad at all times.
2. The coach repeats the process from the other side of the sled after all men have gone through the line.

TYPE OF DRILL: Tackling
NAME OF DRILL: Hit-and-hunt vs the Two-man Sled
TO BE USED BY: Defensive Linemen
PURPOSE: To teach how to deliver a blow and react to the ball carrier
SET UP:

1. Set up two lines in front of the two-man charging sled.
2. Station two ball carriers to the side of the sled, one on each side.
3. The coach stations himself on the sled.

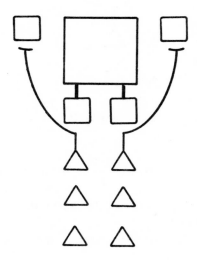

Diagram 6-21.

Instructions:

1. On movement of the coach, the defensive man, from a four-point stance, delivers a blow to the sled.
2. The defensive man may use either a forearm/shoulder-lift or a forearm shiver (Diagram 6-21).
3. After the "hit," the players release to their side and make a form tackle on the ball carrier.
4. After making the tackle the defensive man becomes the ball carrier.

Coaching points:

1. Players should explode out of a four-point stance, stepping with the inside foot.
2. Players should keep head up, back arched, and drive through the sled to the ball carrier.
3. Emphasize quick release after the initial hit.

TYPE OF DRILL: Tackling
NAME OF DRILL: Square-tackling
TO BE USED BY: Defensive Linemen
PURPOSE: To develop tackling technique with emphasis on intensity and balance
SET UP:

1. Place four dummies so that they form a square.
2. Dummies are ten yards apart.
3. Place a ball carrier behind the first dummy and place a tackler in the center of the square.

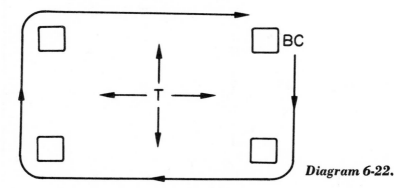

Diagram 6-22.

Instructions:

1. The ball carrier's objective is to run completely around the square without being tackled.
2. The tackler is placed in the middle with his objective being to tackle the ball carrier enroute around the dummies (Diagram 6-22).
3. The tackler stays in the square until he makes a tackle.
4. The ball carrier becomes the tackler on the next play.

Coaching points:

1. Stress staying on the feet running up as close as possible to the ball carrier before tackling him.

TYPE OF DRILL: Tackling
NAME OF DRILL: Beatty-armless-tackling
TO BE USED BY: Linemen
PURPOSE: To teach position and leg-drive for tacklers
SET UP:

1. Set up a ball carrier and a tackler five yards apart.
2. Set this drill up ten yards from the sideline.

Instructions:

1. Ball carrier angles for the sideline.
2. Tackler drives his shoulders into the ball carrier's mid section, keeping the head in front (Diagram 6-23).

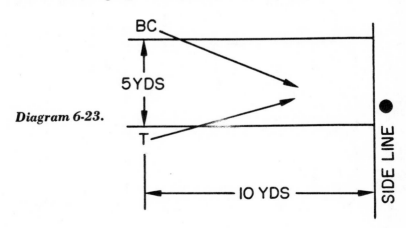

Diagram 6-23.

3. Tackler drives the ball carrier out of bounds.
4. Tackler must maintain strong leg-drive or he will lose contact.

Coaching points:

1. Stress sticking head into ball or numbers as preferred by the coach.
2. After leg-drive and contact is sustained use the same drill, only wrap the arms around the ball carrier.
3. Stress leg-drive and sustained contact.

CHAPTER SEVEN

Winning Drills for the Linebackers

Probably your best football player will be playing the linebacker position because a man in this position has the best opportunity to influence the course of the game.

He must possess exceptional tackling ability because he will be around the ball and in on most tackles. He must possess a great mental attitude because he must lead by example or by aggressive hustle and desire and above all he must be a "hitter."

The linebacking position must be filled with a player who has agility in order to move in pursuit and in pass coverage and he must have the size relative to his opposition.

The linebacker will be called on to do many things. He must be strong enough to neutralize blockers, diagnose plays and get to the ball and yet be able to cover areas vs the pass. Even on occasions he must be able to cover a back coming out of the backfield for a pass.

Several drills are included to cover most phases of the linebacking position and these drills should be added to the drills already being used by the coaching staff.

TYPE OF DRILL: Defensive reaction
NAME OF DRILL: Keying

TO BE USED BY: Linebackers
PURPOSE: To teach linebackers to react to movement
SET UP:

1. Set up a center, two guards and a quarterback on offense.
2. Set up two inside linebackers on defense (Diagram 7-1).

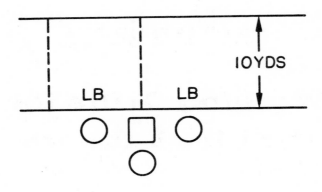

Diagram 7-1.

Instructions:

1. The quarterback will huddle his offensive men and will call "pass" or "run."
2. The guards will fire out at the linebackers on run and set up on a pass call.
3. On the run the linebackers will step up to meet the block of the guards.
4. On pass the linebackers will drop to their zones (center to the normal end position, ten yards deep).
5. On the pass call the quarterback will try to drop the ball in the linebacker zone away from the linebacker.

Coaching points:

1. Two receivers may be added to this drill. They will work on passes in the linebackers' zones.
2. The center is just working on his exchange in this drill. If the coach desires he may place a man in front of the center for additional work.

TYPE OF DRILL: Defensive reaction
NAME OF DRILL: Half-bull
TO BE USED BY: Linebackers
PURPOSE: To teach linebackers to react to a block, regroup and be ready for the next blocker.
SET UP:

1. Set up four blockers in a half circle.
2. Place a linebacker in the middle of the four blockers (Diagram 7-2).
3. The four blockers may use air dummies or arm shields. The linebacker may use arm shields and the blocker live or the whole drill may be live.

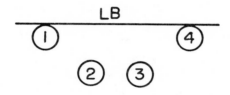

Diagram 7-2.

Instructions:

1. On the command of the coach, the linebacker will assume a football position and chop his feet.
2. The coach will number the blockers, 1-2-3-4 and call one of them to come forward and block the linebacker.
3. The linebacker will shed the blocker with a forearm lift and return to his original position.
4. The coach will then call another blocker who will come forward and use a shoulder block on the linebacker.
5. The linebacker will react once again and regain his original position.
6. This continues until all four men have had a chance to block the linebacker.
7. The players rotate until all have had a chance to be the linebacker.

Coaching points:

1. The coach should impress upon the linebackers that they use both forearms in reacting to the block and keep their feet moving.

TYPE OF DRILL: Defensive reaction
NAME OF DRILL: Bull-in-the-Ring
TO BE USED BY: Linebackers
PURPOSE: To teach linebackers to shed a blocker and to be ready for the next blocker.
SET UP:

1. Place six players around a circle which is five yards in diameter.
2. Place the linebacker inside the circle (Diagram 7-3).

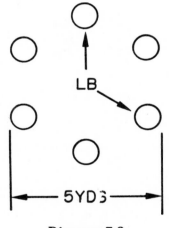

Diagram 7-3.

Instructions:

1. The defensive player, the bull in the middle of the ring, assumes a football position with his feet chopping.
2. On the signal, the coach will call a player and he will enter the circle and try to block the linebacker (the "bull").
3. The linebacker will use a forearm lift on the blocker and set himself for the next blocker.

4. The coach will call another blocker as soon as the first blocker has made contact.
5. This continues until the "bull" has made several hits.
6. The bull should use both forearms depending on the direction of the blocker.

Coaching points:

1. The bull should keep the feet moving at all times and always be ready for a block from any direction.
2. As a safety factor, the coach should make sure that the bull never gets hit from behind.

TYPE OF DRILL: Defensive reaction
NAME OF DRILL: Roll-and-hit
TO BE USED BY: Linebackers
PURPOSE: To teach linebackers to ward off blockers

SET UP:

1. Set up two lines of blockers, five yards apart.
2. Set the linebacker in the middle of the two lines and five yards away.

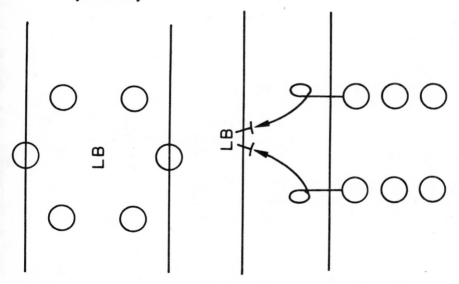

Diagram 7-4.

Instructions:

1. On the signal from the coach, the first man in the right line does a forward roll and tries to block the linebacker as he comes out of the roll (Diagram 7-4).
2. The linebacker uses a forearm lift on the blocker and tries to catch him just as he comes out of the roll.
3. As contact is made, the blocker from the left line does a forward roll and tries to block the linebacker as soon as he gets out of the roll.
4. The linebacker uses a left–right forearm lift on the blocker. The linebacker will alternate arms for the forearm lift.
5. This drill proceeds until the linebacker has taken about four or five shots.
6. The linebacker then gets in one of the lines and the blocker becomes the linebacker.

Coaching points:

1. The coach must time the drill so that the blockers come at the linebacker one at a time.
2. The linebacker should use a right forearm lift on the line to his right and a left forearm lift on the line to his left. He should keep his feet chopping and be in a good football position.

TYPE OF DRILL: Defensive reaction
NAME OF DRILL: Mirror
TO BE USED BY: Linebackers
PURPOSE: To teach linebackers to ward off blockers and keep their eyes on the ball carrier
SET UP:

1. Set up four standing dummies with holders.
2. Set up one line of ball carriers.
3. Set up one line of tacklers.

Instructions:

1. On the signal from the coach, the ball carrier will dodge in and out of the four dummies. They can go back and forth if

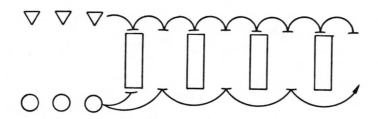

Diagram 7-5.

they desire, the objective being to cut up one of the holes without being tackled (Diagram 7-5).

2. The defensive lineman will be in a good football position and keep in front of the ball carrier. Every time the defensive man passes a dummy he should use a forearm lift or shiver on the dummy.

3. The tackle should be made before the ball carrier crosses the line.

Coaching points:

1. The tackler assumes that the dummies are linemen who are coming out to block him, so he must ward them off to get to the ball carrier.

2. The tackler should not overrun the ball carrier and should be in position to make contact at any time.

3. This drill may be used with a "form" tackle.

4. The coach may place dummies on the ground for the defensive man to jump over. This would be in the second phase of the drill.

TYPE OF DRILL: Defensive reaction
NAME OF DRILL: Scramble-drill vs the Sled
TO BE USED BY: Linebackers
PURPOSE: To teach a linebacker to react to a ball carrier after working on one of the following defensive techniques: forearm lift, forearm shiver, spin-out, seat-roll

SET UP:

1. Line up players on the second pad of the seven-man sled.
2. Use both ends of the sled.
3. Line up ball carriers in front of the third pad facing the linebacker.
4. Coach stations himself in the center of the sled, between the linebackers.
5. Place two dummies on their side at each end of the sled.

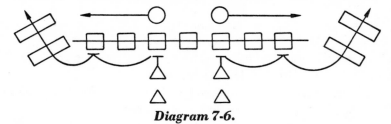

Diagram 7-6.

Instructions:

1. The coach will alternate working right and left.
2. The linebacker will line up on the second pad, and the coach will designate the defensive technique to be used.
3. The linebacker will deliver a blow on the second pad, carry out his maneuver, hit the last pad, carry out his maneuver, search for the ball carrier, step over the dummies that are lying on the ground and make a form tackle on the ball carrier (Diagram 7-6).

Coaching points:

1. The ball carrier should be set in such a position so that the linebacker has a chance to make the tackle.
2. The coach should continue this drill until all players have had a chance at each end of the sled as well as becoming the ball carrier.

TYPE OF DRILL: Warding off blockers
NAME OF DRILL: Billy-goat
TO BE USED BY: Linebackers
PURPOSE: To teach linebacker to ward off blockers, control his area and make the tackle

SET UP:

1. Set up a center, quarterback, a blocker, running back and a linebacker.
2. Set up markers to simulate the dive hole.
3. The coach may set up two groups and alternate right and left.

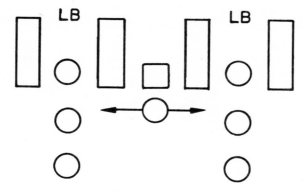

Diagram 7-7.

Instructions:

1. On the snap, the quarterback will hand off to the running back on a dive play.
2. The blocker will fire out at the linebacker and try to clear the hole (Diagram 7-7).
3. The linebacker will close the hole, make contact, shed the blocker and make the tackle.

Coaching points:

1. The tackle should be made as close to the line of scrimmage as possible.
2. The coach may alternate right and left.
3. The blockers and the linebackers alternate positions.
4. If running backs are used they should try to break the tackle and sprint ten yards up field.

TYPE OF DRILL: Warding off blocker while pursuing
NAME OF DRILL: Scrape

TO BE USED BY: Linebackers
PURPOSE: To teach linebackers to ward off blockers as
                        they pursue to the outside
SET UP:

1. Set up four markers two yards apart.
2. Set up two players as dummy holders in the first two holes
   and a ball carrier in the third hole.
3. Make two set-ups so that the linebackers learn to move left
   and right.

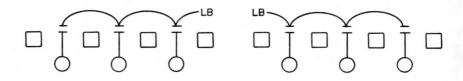

Diagram 7-8.

Instructions:

1. On the signal from the coach the linebacker moves down
   the line using a forearm lift on the blockers.
2. The blockers (dummy holders) come across the line and
   take a good shot at the linebacker.
3. When the linebacker gets to the third hole he form tackles
   the ball carrier (Diagram 7-8).
4. A variation of this drill could be to have the ball carrier
   start behind the first blocker and finally cut up the third
   hole.

Coaching points:

1. Coach should stress good body position with feet chopping.
2. Linebacker should use inside shoulder and forearm on
   blockers and should alternate so that he moves both ways.
3. The linebacker's head should be "across the bow" when he
   makes the tackle.

TYPE OF DRILL: Form tackling

NAME OF DRILL: Mazzucco-bump
TO BE USED BY: Linebackers
PURPOSE: To teach linebackers to keep proper position on the ball carrier and to be in a good football position upon contact

SET UP:

1. Set up four markers, two yards apart, a ball carrier with a light dummy and a linebacker.
2. Make two set-ups so that more players may get into the action.
3. Coach stations himself between the two groups.

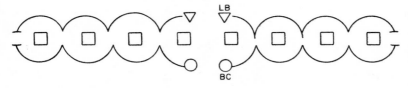

Diagram 7-9.

Instructions:

1. Ball carrier, holding a light dummy, dips into each hole and then repeats the process coming back.
2. The linebacker meets the ball carrier in each hole, makes a form tackle and proceeds to the next hole. The linebacker just takes one shot at the ball carrier and moves to the next hole quickly (Diagram 7-9).
3. The ball carrier must make an honest effort at each hole.
4. Drill should be started at half speed and then the tempo can be picked up as the drill is mastered.

Coaching points:

1. Coach should stress good football position when the linebacker makes contact, knees flexed, head up, arms wrapped around the ball carrier.

TYPE OF DRILL: Rhythm and hit
NAME OF DRILL: Little-bull
TO BE USED BY: Linebackers

PURPOSE: To develop arm and leg action while delivering a blow

SET UP:

1. Set up two offensive men in a good football position, one
yard apart.
2. Place the linebacker in the center, facing the two offensive
men about two yards away.

Diagram 7-10.

Instructions:

1. The blocker on the right steps forward and the linebacker
uses a right forearm lift while stepping with his right foot.
2. The blocker on the left steps forward and the linebacker
uses a left forearm lift while stepping with his left foot
(Diagram 7-10).
3. Repeat the process until the linebacker has made three hits
to each side.

Coaching points:

1. The coach should stress timing and rhythm for this drill.
2. The blocker that is waiting should not move forward until
the linebacker returns to his original position.

TYPE OF DRILL: Tackling
NAME OF DRILL: Tennessee-Shadow
TO BE USED BY: Linebackers
PURPOSE: To teach a linebacker how to keep a ball
carrier from scoring

SET UP:

1. Set up a linebacker and a ball carrier in a five yard square.
2. One of the boundaries should be the goal line.

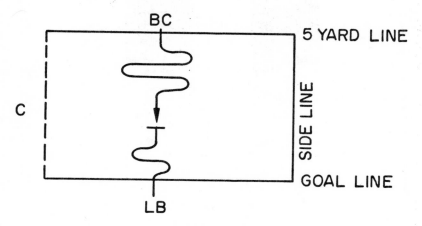

Diagram 7-11.

Instructions:

1. Linebacker lines up on the goal line.
2. Ball carrier lines up on the five-yard line.
3. Ball carrier moves back and forth in his square trying to get over the goal line.
4. Linebacker shadows the ball carrier and tries to keep him from scoring (Diagram 7-11).

Coaching points:

1. This should be a competitive drill in that the linebacker must keep the ball carrier from getting in to the end zone. If he does score the linebacker has to try again.
2. A tackle over the line is six points so all tackles have to be made out of the end zone.

TYPE OF DRILL: Read and react
NAME OF DRILL: Linebacker-one-on-one
TO BE USED BY: Linebackers
PURPOSE: To teach a linebacker to react to a blocker and to force a ball carrier
SET UP:

1. Set up a blocker, linebacker and ball carrier.
2. Mark the area with dummies as diagrammed.
3. Linebacker is 3 yards off the ball.

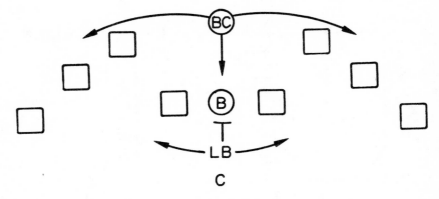

Diagram 7-12.

Instructions:

1. The linebacker uses a forearm flipper if the blocker is coming straight at him.
2. The linebacker uses his hands if the blocker is trying to take him in or out.
3. The ball carrier uses the dummies for his cuts.
4. The linebacker forces the ball carrier outside (Diagram 7-12).

Coaching points:

1. The ball carrier may come straight up the middle to keep the linebacker honest.
2. The linebacker should form-tackle the ball carrier as this is a reaction drill rather than a tackling drill.

TYPE OF DRILL: Form tackling
NAME OF DRILL: Shed-and-tackle
TO BE USED BY: Linebackers
PURPOSE: To teach linebackers to shed the blockers and to react to the ball carrier

SET UP:

1. Set up two blockers and a ball carrier facing the linebacker. Linebackers alternate positions, i.e. they become blockers and ball carriers.

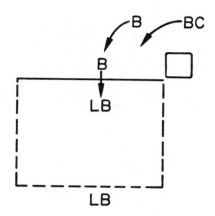

Diagram 7-13.

Instructions:

1. Linebacker assumes his position in his linebacking area.
2. First blocker attacks the linebacker trying to drive him out of his area.
3. Linebacker squares up on the blocker, uses a forearm flip, disengages the blocker, comes up square, repeats the process with the next blocker and finally makes a form tackle on the ball carrier (Diagram 7-13).

Coaching points:

1. Time of the blockers and ball carrier is important. Obviously they cannot all come at the same time.
2. The linebacker may use arm shields.

TYPE OF DRILL: Tackling
NAME OF DRILL: Dummy-dropper
TO BE USED BY: Linebackers
PURPOSE: To develop good balance while keeping the eyes open and the head up
SET UP:

1. Set up a ball carrier, linebacker and three men holding dummies.

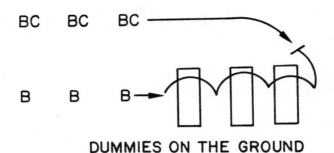

DUMMIES ON THE GROUND

Diagram 7-14.

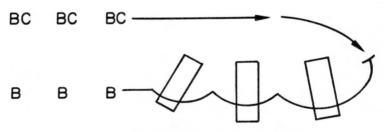

PLAYERS DROPPING DUMMIES

Diagram 7-15.

Instructions:

1. During the first part of the drill the linebacker steps over the dummies that are lying on the ground and form tackles the ball carrier (Diagram 7-14).
2. The second phase the players hold the dummies and may or may not drop them on the ground (Diagram 7-15).
3. The linebacker must work over the dummies keeping the head up, shoulders square, hips square, while high-stepping over the dummies.
4. The linebacker will get the "feel" of the dummies on the ground and will not look down at them.
5. The dummies on the ground simulate a blocker who has been knocked down etc.

Coaching points:

1. The players holding the dummies can drop them at will. There is no set pattern. They must, however give the linebacker time to react.

TYPE OF DRILL: Reaction
NAME OF DRILL: Linebacker-three-on-one
TO BE USED BY: Linebackers
PURPOSE: To acquaint the backer with the blocking schemes he will have to contend with

SET UP:

1. Set up three offensive linemen facing the linebacker.

DOWN BLOCK

C-G CROSS BLOCK

G-T CROSS BLOCK

Diagram 7-16.

Instructions:

1. The coach will stand behind the linebacker and direct the offensive blocks (Diagram 7-16).
2. Other schemes may be added such as pass reaction, one-on-one or double-team.

Coaching points:

1. Linebacker should be in a hitting position with his feet churning.
2. Should have shoulders square and ready to use either arm to ward off blocks.

TYPE OF DRILL: Reading and reacting
NAME OF DRILL: Guard-reaction
TO BE USED BY: Inside Linebackers
PURPOSE: To teach linebackers to read the block of the offensive guard and to react to the ball

SET UP:

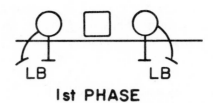

Ist PHASE

Diagram 7-17.

1st phase: center, two guards and linebackers.

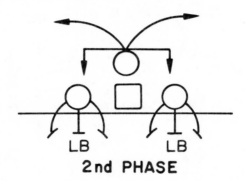

2nd PHASE

Diagram 7-18.

2nd phase: center, two guards, linebackers and quarterback.

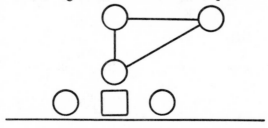

LB   LB
3rd PHASE
Diagram 7-19.

3rd phase: center, two guards, linebackers, quarterback and backs.

Instructions:

1. First Phase: the offensive guard will make a straight out block or reach block (Diagram 7-17).
   The linebacker will:
   A. Keep his inside hand free.
   B. Straight block. The backer takes blocker on with inside flipper keeping shoulders square.
   C. On reach block. Backer always takes a lateral step first then a cross-over and takes the blocker on with the inside arm.
2. Second Phase: The linebacker must begin to read the ball (Diagram 7-18).
   A. On reach block it may not be necessary to take on the block. Depends on the action of the quarterback.
   B. On plays away when the linebacker is being cut off, he drops steps, crosses over and then gets into pursuit.
3. Third Phase: The backs are added (Diagram 7-19).
   A. The linebacker reads through the guard to the action of the backs.

Coaching points:

1. The first phase should be used until the linebackers get the feel of the guard. The 2nd and 3rd phase should be added accordingly.
2. The linebacker must learn to read the whole situation rather than just keying the guard, quarterback or the backs.

TYPE OF DRILL: Pass defense reaction
NAME OF DRILL: My-ball
TO BE USED BY: Linebackers
PURPOSE: To teach linebackers to fight for the ball
SET UP:

1. Two lines of linebackers face the coach. They are five yards apart and ten yards from the coach.

Instructions:

1. The coach throws the ball between the two lines (Diagram 7-20).

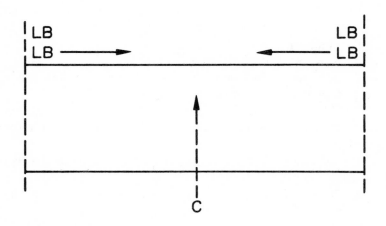

Diagram 7-20.

2. The linebackers rush the ball and try to catch it at its highest point.
3. The coach should vary the throws and even throw it in the direction of one of the linebackers on occasion.

Coaching points:

1. If this is a live drill, the linebacker who does not catch the ball becomes a tackler.
2. This is an aggressive drill and should be used only sparingly.
3. Players should be taught how to use their body in going for the ball. It is much the same technique as teaching a player to rebound in basketball. Body position becomes important.

TYPE OF DRILL: Pass defense reaction
NAME OF DRILL: Twenty-catch
TO BE USED BY: Linebackers
PURPOSE: To develop hand-eye coordination
SET UP:

1. Linebackers line up in a straight line facing the coach.

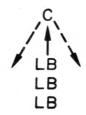

Diagram 7-21.

Instructions:

1. This is a simple warm up drill to teach the linebackers to catch the ball, tuck it in and take off up field.
2. Linebackers come toward the coach and he throws the ball a different way each time the linebacker comes up again (Diagram 7-21).
3. The four different ways are:
   1—Straight
   2—Behind
   3—Over
   4—Out
4. This is done to both sides, then stress catching the ball with one hand.

Coaching points:

1. When the ball is thrown behind the linebacker, he must roll his hips around just like he is covering a curl.
2. On the "out" the linebacker should get the ball on the break.

TYPE OF DRILL: Pass defense reaction
NAME OF DRILL: Tennessee-backer
TO BE USED BY: Linebackers
PURPOSE: To teach a linebacker to get back in his zone on the reaction of the quarterback and to intercept or knock the pass down
SET UP:

1. Set up a quarterback, linebacker and a receiver.
2. Set the receiver ten yards down field.

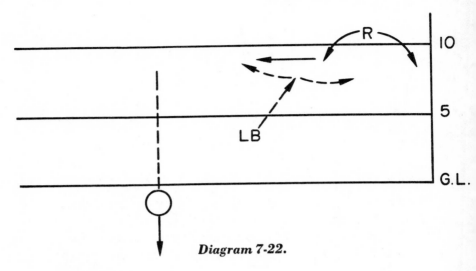

Diagram 7-22.

Instructions:

1. Quarterback drops back to pass.
2. Linebacker drops to his zone.
3. Quarterback throws an inside curl, outside curl or slide in pattern (Diagram 7-22).
4. Receiver will signal the route to the quarterback.

Coaching points:

1. At first most of the passes will be completed but the linebacker will be surprised as to how much ground he can cover.

TYPE OF DRILL: Pass defense
NAME OF DRILL: Tip
TO BE USED BY: Linebackers
PURPOSE: To teach a linebacker to catch a deflected ball
SET UP:

1. Players line up: Front tip drill—facing the coach
                            Angle tip drill—right angles to the coach
                            Double tip drill—two lines facing the coach

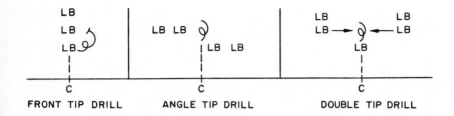

Diagram 7-23.

Instructions:

1. The coach throws the ball to the nearest linebacker who "tips the ball."
2. The nearest linebacker must catch the ball before it hits the ground (Diagram 7-23).
3. The tipper becomes the receiver the next time around.

Coaching points:

1. The ball should be thrown over the tipper's head at times to keep the defender alert.
2. If the drill is held during a live practice a little incentive may be added by having the man who tipped the ball turn and tackle the receiver. If it is not live, the tipper can form tackle the receiver.

TYPE OF DRILL: Pass reaction
NAME OF DRILL: Hand-and-eye-coordination
TO BE USED BY: Linebackers
PURPOSE: To teach linebackers to react to the ball
SET UP:

1. The linebacker lines up with his back to the coach who is ten yards away.

Instructions:

1. Coach calls "ball" and throws it to the side in which the linebacker turns.

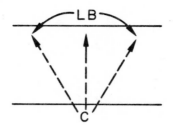

Diagram 7-24.

2. Linebacker must react to and catch the ball (Diagram 7-24).
3. Linebacker should learn to turn both ways.

Coaching points:

1. The linebacker runs the ball to the coach and returns to the line.
2. After the drill is mastered, the coach may call "ball" and throw it to either side of the linebacker. The linebacker must react to the ball.
3. Ball should be thrown easy to make the drill equitable.

TYPE OF DRILL: Short zone coverage
NAME OF DRILL: Through-a-man-to-the-ball
TO BE USED BY: Linebackers
PURPOSE: To teach a linebacker to play the ball at its highest arc and to go through the receivers to the ball

SET UP:

1. Linebackers assume normal linebacking position in a marked area.
2. The quarterback and two receivers (in the tight end positions) line up on the line of scrimmage.

Instructions:

1. The quarterback tells the receivers what pattern to run.

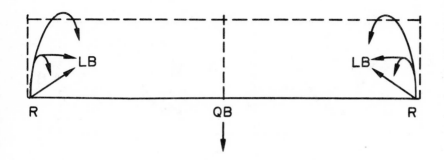

Diagram 7-25.

    Hook, curl, slant-in, slant-out. Any pattern may be used as long as it is designed for the linebacker zone area.

2. On command the receivers run the patterns that are called. The linebackers drop to their zone and react to the ball (Diagram 7-25).

3. The emphasis should be on the incomplete or the intercepted pass. That is, this is a defensive drill primarily.

Coaching points:

1. The drill is more meaningful if the linebackers' zones are marked. The linebacker then gets a "feel" of his zone.

2. The linebackers should learn to use their body in going for the ball.

TYPE OF DRILL: Pass defense reaction
NAME OF DRILL: Bad-ball
TO BE USED BY: Linebackers
PURPOSE: To teach a linebacker to react to a poorly thrown pass
SET UP:

1. Linebackers line up in their normal position facing the quarterback.

2. Linebacker's zone should be marked

Instructions:

1. The quarterback (coach) will drop back to pass and the

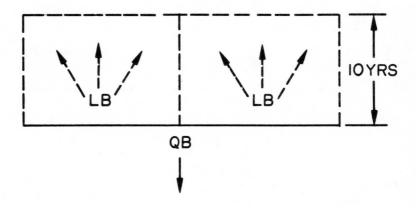

Diagram 7-26.

    linebacker will drop to his zone coverage.

2. The quarterback purposely tries to throw the ball away from the linebacker while trying to keep the ball in his zone.

3. Quarterback alternates zones. While one linebacker is re-trieving the ball the quarterback throws to the other zone (Diagram 7-26).

4. The linebacker tries to catch every ball before it hits the ground.

Coaching points:

1. The quarterback must not make this too tough but should try to throw the ball that can be caught with some effort on the linebacker's part.

TYPE OF DRILL: Pass reaction
NAME OF DRILL: Zone Coverage
TO BE USED BY: Linebackers
PURPOSE: To teach a linebacker to get in the proper position in his zone before the quarterback throws the ball

SET UP:

1. Linebackers take their normal position in a marked-off area.

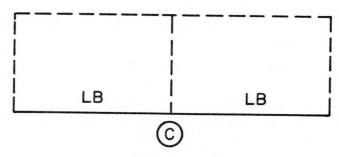

Diagram 7-27.

Instructions:

1. The quarterback or coach assumes his normal position and on command (See Diagram 7-28):

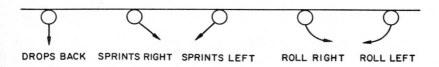

DROPS BACK   SPRINTS RIGHT   SPRINTS LEFT   ROLL RIGHT   ROLL LEFT

Diagram 7-28.

2. Linebacker drops immediately to his pre-determined area (pre-determined by the type of defense to be used).
3. Quarterback may come back on a simulated draw play just to keep the backers honest. The backers must react to the draw.

Coaching points:

1. The area should be marked off, ten yards deep and the normal width of the linebacker zone in order for the linebacker to get the feel of his area.
2. The coach should designate potential receivers such as the tight end, and go over areas of responsibility with the linebackers before starting the drill.

TYPE OF DRILL: Pass reaction
NAME OF DRILL: Lateral-movement

TO BE USED BY: Linebackers
PURPOSE: To teach lateral movement in pass defense
SET UP:

   1. Linebackers line up facing the coach.

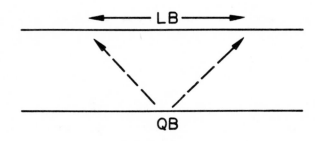

Diagram 7-29.

Instructions:

1. On command the linebacker assumes a football position
   with his feet churning.
2. The linebacker reacts to the movement off the quarterback's
   arm, moving laterally along the line (Diagram 7-29).
3. The quarterback fakes a couple of times and then throws
   the ball.
4. The linebacker receives the ball at its highest arc and runs
   the ball back to the quarterback.

Coaching points:

1. The quarterback must get the linebacker moving laterally
   a few times before he throws the ball.
2. The linebacker must be able to change direction quickly
   and get to the ball as quick as he can after the ball is
   thrown.

TYPE OF DRILL: Pass defense reaction
NAME OF DRILL: Catching-in-a-crowd
TO BE USED BY: Linebackers
PURPOSE: To teach linebackers to intercept the ball in
                                    a congested area

SET UP:

1. Linebackers form in a group, facing the coach who is twenty yards away.
2. Two or three footballs are needed for this drill.

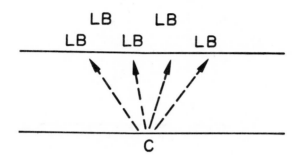

Diagram 7-30.

Instructions:

1. The coach throws the ball into the "crowd." The linebacker who catches the ball returns it to the coach (Diagram 7-30).
2. The drill progresses until all linebackers have caught a ball.
3. Players who have returned the ball to the coach, kneel down by the coach and shout encouragement to the rest of the group.

Coaching points:

1. This is a highly competitive drill and very dangerous.
2. This drill should only be used at the end of the pass reaction drills.
3. It is a high morale drill.
4. Basically nothing technical is accomplished with this drill except the coach can easily spot his best pass defender.

TYPE OF DRILL: Reaction to the ball
NAME OF DRILL: Fumble-drill-and-reaction
TO BE USED BY: Linebackers
PURPOSE: To teach a linebacker to release a blocker and react to a fumble

SET UP:

1. The linebacker assumes a football position in front of a down lineman.
2. The coach lines up five yards behind the down lineman.

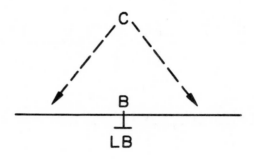

Diagram 7-31.

Instructions:

1. On the command "hit" the lineman charges out at the linebacker and tries to drive him back (Diagram 7-31).
2. The linebacker makes contact with the blocker, controls him.
3. The coach flips the ball right or left and the backer disengages the blocker and reacts to the fumble.

Coaching points:

1. The coach should vary his timing in releasing the ball.

TYPE OF DRILL: Pass defense reaction
NAME OF DRILL: Running-the-line
TO BE USED BY: Linebackers
PURPOSE: To develop backward running and change of direction

SET UP:

1. Linebackers face the coach on a yard stripe. A net behind the linebackers saves time on the drill.

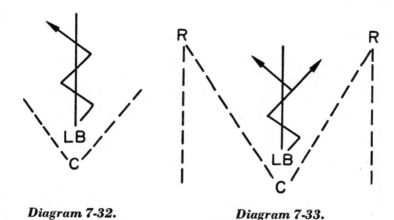

Diagram 7-32.　　　　　　**Diagram 7-33.**

Instructions:

1. Linebackers run backwards then react to the ball and start up field.
2. Linebacker will roll hips right or left depending on the action of the quarterback.
3. The quarterback will also incorporate the bad pass drill so that the linebacker will be able to react to the deflected or badly thrown ball (Diagram 7-32).
4. Next we have the linebacker get back into his area, break down into a good football position and the ball will be thrown to one side or the other in his area (Diagram 7-33).
5. Two receivers are placed on either side of the line about 15 yards apart. The quarterback will throw to either receiver and the linebacker must be able to cover the whole area.

Coaching points:

1. This is a must drill every day for linebackers. It should follow the twenty-catch drill.

TYPE OF DRILL: Tackling
NAME OF DRILL: Eye-opener
TO BE USED BY: Linebackers
PURPOSE: To teach linebacker to "read" direction.
                   Helps linebackers develop a nose for the ball

SET UP:

1. Set up six markers to simulate offensive holes.
2. Number the holes.
3. Set up a ball carrier with a light bag or shield.
4. Set up a linebacker opposite the ball carrier.

Instructions:

1. Coach designates the hole that the ball carrier will run.
2. Linebacker turns his back to the ball carrier.
3. On the signal from the coach the ball carrier will drive up the hole designated and the linebacker will turn and react to movement (Diagram 7-34).
4. The variation of the drill would be to use a lead blocker through the hole.
5. The linebacker form-tackles the ball carrier who runs with a light dummy.

Coaching points:

1. Coach should look for quickness in the linebacker locating the ball.
2. Coach should stress proper form in meeting the ball carrier.

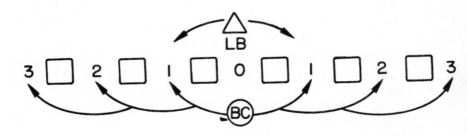

Diagram 7-34.

CHAPTER EIGHT

Winning Drills
for the Center

It is a common feeling among coaches, that the "center" position is probably the most important position on the offensive line. He handles the ball on every play which will average between forty and sixty times a game.

The center must be able to make a good exchange with the quarterback in the T formation, plus he must be able to center the ball for punts, point after touchdowns and field goals. In addition to the above he is called upon to be a full-time blocker.

In light of all this the center is probably the most under-coached lineman on the squad. The reason for this is that his practice time is so diversified; he must work with the backs when they are timing plays; he must work with the line when they are working on blocking or vs various defensive formations and yet he must find the time to work with the kicking game. To add to this confusion, the center, on small squads, will probably be a linebacker and will have to work on this phase of the game.

When the coach evaluates his personnel he usually chooses the center first. He looks for an athlete who has good size, better than average agility and a fierce competitor. The center must be a leader and a hustler because the whole team revolves around his enthusiasm.

It is an oddity, that with such an important position, that there is very little written about the center position.

TYPE OF DRILL: Offensive
NAME OF DRILL: Center-warm-up
TO BE USED BY: Centers
PURPOSE: To teach the center the proper method of stretching and warming up procedures
SET UP:

   1. Have the centers face the coach (Diagram 8-1).

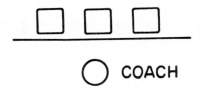

Diagram 8-1.

Instructions:

   1. Center stands with right foot over the left and "bounces" down touching the ground on the tenth count.
   2. Center stands with left foot over the right and bounces down touching the ground on the tenth count.
   3. Center spreads his legs as far apart as possible and bounces down placing his head on the ground on the tenth count.
   4. Center spreads his legs as far apart as possible and touches left hand to right toe, comes up to the starting position and touches the right hand to the left toe. This is alternated for ten counts.
   5. Center spreads his legs as far apart as possible and rotates his body in a circular motion.

Coaching points:

   1. The above exercises are designed to strengthen and stretch the hamstring and quadricep muscles.

2. It also gives the center flexibility from his "stance" position.

TYPE OF DRILL: Offensive
NAME OF DRILL: Stance-warm-up
TO BE USED BY: The center
PURPOSE: To teach the center how to obtain good bal-
                 ance
SET UP:

1. Set up the centers facing the coach.

Instructions:

1. The center assumes a well-balanced stance without a ball.
   A. The coach approaches each center and pushes or pulls
      him trying to throw him off balance. If the center is
      easily moved then he should re-adjust his feet.
   B. The coach has the center block straight ahead, the
      coach catches the center. If the center takes a jab step
      or has trouble moving in a natural movement then
      adjustment is necessary.
   C. The coach has the center simulate a right and left block
      and makes the adjustment as above.
2. The center assumes a well-balanced stance with a ball and
   snaps the ball to the coach. The coach will direct the center
   to move straight, right or left and will check his balance
   and movement.

Coaching points:

1. This is to be used as a fundamental drill before blocking
   dummies or live contact is used.
2. The center must learn that his first responsibility is to center
   the ball first. All else is secondary.

TYPE OF DRILL: Offensive
NAME OF DRILL: Center's-stance
TO BE USED BY: The center
PURPOSE: To teach and perfect the fundamental stance
                 of the center

SET UP:

1. Set up the centers facing the coach.
2. The coach will direct the centers as follows:

Instructions:

1. Feet parallel, heels approximately two inches off the ground. Weight on balls of feet. Feet pointed straight forward.
2. Knees are flexed and on line with the stance.
3. Hips should be a little higher than the shoulders so that the quarterback does not have to reach down for the ball. This will vary with the size of the center and the size of the quarterback.
4. The shoulders should be squared with the line of scrimmage and the head should be up in a "bulled neck" fashion.
5. The right arm is extended and the right hand grasps the ball with the fingers spread on the laces. Actual position depends on the size of the center's hand.
6. The left arm is straight down and locked at the elbow. Some coaches prefer to have this hand on the ground and some prefer to have this hand on the lower end of the ball.

Coaching points:

1. The weight should be evenly distributed and not too much weight should be on the ball. The center must be able to move right and left as well as straight ahead so his weight should be balanced.

TYPE OF DRILL: Offensive
NAME OF DRILL: Center-quarterback-exchange
TO BE USED BY: Centers and quarterbacks
PURPOSE: To teach the techniques for a proper T formation exchange

SET UP:

1. Set up the centers and quarterbacks facing the coach (Diagram 8-2).
2. Coach will teach and review methods for the proper exchange.

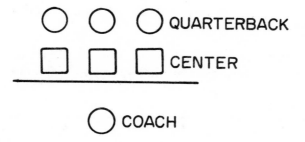

Diagram 8-2.

Instructions:

1. Exchange without using a ball:
   A. The quarterback will place his hand under the center at the exact position that he desires to receive the ball.
   B. The center swings his hand up and slaps the quarterback's hand. The hand will turn in a normal rotation so that the palms of the center and quarterback will meet.
2. Reverse exchange:
   A. The quarterback will place the ball under the center in the exact position that he desires to receive it.
   B. The center will reach up and take the ball from the quarterback and place it on the ground.
2. Actual exchange:
   A. The center will snap the ball placing it in the quarterback's hands.
   B. This maneuver must be done several times before the exact position is reached.

Coaching points:

1. The quarterback must put "pressure" on the center so that he knows exactly where his hand is.
2. The ball should come up as hard and as fast as possible.

TYPE OF DRILL: Offensive
NAME OF DRILL: Exchange-drill-vs-sled
TO BE USED BY: Centers and quarterbacks

PURPOSE: To perfect the center-quarterback exchange
                        while working on proper get-off

SET UP:

1. Set up three centers, three quarterbacks in front of alternate
   pads of the seven man charging sled (Diagram 8-3).

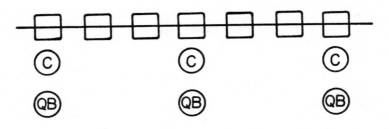

Diagram 8-3.

Instructions:

1. The quarterbacks will alternate calling the cadence and the
   centers will snap the ball and fire out at the sled.
2. The progression should be for the quarterback to call the
   shoulder to be used by the center and the maneuver to be
   used by the quarterback. For example: "Left shoulder,
   reverse pivot on three," the center will snap the ball, hit the
   pad with the left shoulder and the quarterbacks will all do
   a reverse pivot to the left.
3. The centers should rotate after each call so that the center
   has a chance to work with all quarterbacks.

Coaching points:

1. The coach should be concerned with the timing of the drill.
   Each snap should come up at the same time and each center
   should hit the sled at the same time.
2. This drill should be used daily especially in the early season
   practice sessions.

TYPE OF DRILL: Offensive
NAME OF DRILL: Alternating
TO BE USED BY: Centers

PURPOSE: To work on the center quarterback exchange
                            plus blocking when only centers are avail-
                            able
SET UP:

1. Three centers are needed for this drill. If only two are available the coach will act as the quarterback.
2. Set up three centers, one as a defensive man, one as the
   center and one as the quarterback (Diagram 8-4).

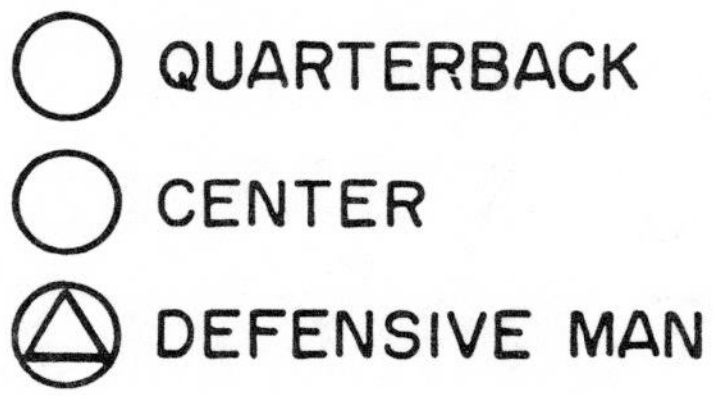

◯ QUARTERBACK

◯ CENTER

△ DEFENSIVE MAN

Diagram 8-4.

Instructions:

1. The coach will show the centers how the quarterback receives the ball.
2. One center will act as a defensive man, one as the center
   and one will act as the quarterback.
3. On the command from the "quarterback" the center will
   snap the ball and fire out blocking the defensive man.
4. The defensive man may play head-on or right or left of the
   center and should try to reach the quarterback.
5. The quarterback may also show pass so that the center can
   work on his pass blocking.
6. The players will rotate after each drill so that they work in
   each position.

Coaching points:

1. The emphasis must be on a good snap first and then the
   block.
2. The defensive man may use a dummy instead of live until
   all the fundamentals are mastered.

TYPE OF DRILL: Offensive
NAME OF DRILL: Fundamentals-of-blocking
TO BE USED BY: Centers
PURPOSE: To teach the center to master the funda-
                        mental blocking techniques
SET UP:

1. The centers line up with the other linemen who are learn-
   ing the various offensive blocks.
2. The center will always have a ball, and center to another
   center before making the block (Diagram 8-5).

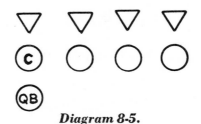

Diagram 8-5.

Instructions:

1. The center must master all the fundamental blocks which
   include the shoulder blocks, near-foot, near-shoulder, reverse shoulder (to a crab), reach and scramble and pass
   protection.
2. While working with the linemen on these fundamental
   blocks the centers will always work together, so that one
   can be a quarterback and receive the ball.
3. This is important because by receiving the ball, the center
   becomes conscious of how important a good snap is. Once
   he, acting as quarterback, receives a few snaps he will improve his own techniques.
4. In essence the centers coach each other.

Coaching points:

1. A center should never make an exchange or work on any
   phase of the game without a man in front of him or a man
   to receive the ball.

2. Conversely, if the center is working with the backs on timing he should have another center in front of him.

TYPE OF DRILL: Offensive
NAME OF DRILL: Wrist-snap
TO BE USED BY: Centers
PURPOSE: To teach the centers how to snap the ball for punts, PAT's and field goals
SET UP:

1. Have centers pair off (Diagram 8-6).

Diagram 8-6.   Diagram 8-7.

Instructions:

1. The center will assume his stance for a punt snap.
2. He will straighten up, without changing his hand position and raise the ball over his head (Diagram 8-7).
3. The center will then pass the ball to his partner with his hands extended over his head.
4. This drill should be started at five yards distance and progress to fifteen yards.
5. If the center is having trouble reaching his partner or having trouble spiraling the ball then he should change his hand position.
6. Both hands should be used in this drill, one as the passing hand and one as the guiding hand.

Coaching points:

1. This drill should be done every day for at least ten or fifteen times.
2. The player should not change his hand position or foot position when he raises up.

TYPE OF DRILL: Offensive
NAME OF DRILL: Centering-for-the-punt
TO BE USED BY: Centers
PURPOSE: To teach the fundamentals of centering for the punt

SET UP:

1. Set up the centers so that they are back to back about fifteen yards apart (Diagram 8-8).

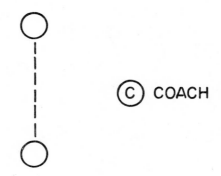

Diagram 8-8.

Instructions:

1. The coach instructs the center on which stance to use.
2. The feet are staggered, that is if the center is right-handed, his right toe will be even with the instep of the left foot.
3. The center passes the ball to the coach and without changing his feet, bends over and uses this as his stance.
4. The right hand grips the laces just as in a pass and the left hand is placed on the back of the ball as a guide.
5. The centers snap the ball back and forth adjusting so that they perfect the snap.

6. This should be done every day with the coach's supervision.

Coaching points:

1. Centering for the punt has become a lost art with the advent of the T formation, hence much extra work must be spent on this phase of the game. It could mean a ball game.

TYPE OF DRILL: Offensive
NAME OF DRILL: Arm-and-wrist-strength
TO BE USED BY: Centers
PURPOSE: To strengthen the wrist and arm action of the center
SET UP:

1. Centers pair off and work together with a weighted football.

Instructions:

1. The Voit Power Arm Football is expressly designed for centers and passers. It is a regulation size football only it weighs about five pounds. It is the same idea as the medicine ball in basketball.
2. Centers should warm up with this ball by playing catch at a distance of about five yards.
3. They should then drop to one knee and continue playing catch.
4. The next progression would be to then use the overhead wrist snap.
5. Finally they should center to each other, starting at five yards and working back.

Coaching points:

1. This weighted ball should be part of the center's equipment especially during the summer months.

TYPE OF DRILL: Offensive
NAME OF DRILL: Speed-and-snap
TO BE USED BY: Centers
PURPOSE: To develop wrist action for speed in the long snap

SET UP:

1. Centers pair off seven yards apart and progress to fifteen yards apart.

Instructions:

1. Centers get down on one knee, right knee if they are right-handed, left knee if they are left-handed.
2. Ball is placed on the ground. The center takes a proper grip on the ball and raises it over his head and passes it to his teammate.
3. Centers try to snap the ball with their wrists rather than using too much arm.
4. Centers then assume their proper stance. They raise the ball off the ground about six inches and snap the ball from this position. Note: most of the accuracy comes from the opposite hand but in this drill the center tries to develop as much accuracy with one hand as possible.

Coaching points:

1. Since the success of the punting game depends on a good, fast, accurate snap, we suggest that this drill be incorporated each day, usually before or after practice.

TYPE OF DRILL: Offensive
NAME OF DRILL: Tire
TO BE USED BY: Centers
PURPOSE: To teach centers accuracy while working on the kicking game

SET UP:

1. Hang tires from the goal posts or some suitable cross bar.
2. Have the tires at various lengths so they may be used for other drills.
3. A net may be used with markers attached so that they may be used as a target (Diagram 8-9).

Instructions:

1. This is an old-fashioned but good drill and can be used as an early work function or after practice.

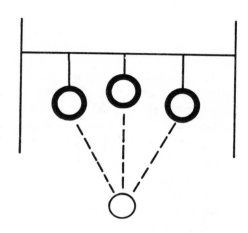

Diagram 8-9.

2. The center should start with the over-head flip from five, ten and fifteen yards as a warm-up.
3. The center then assumes his stance for the kicking game and tries to hit the target. He should start from five yards and progress to fifteen yards.
4. If another center is available he can flip the ball back to the center using an over-head flip technique.
5. If only one center is available he should have at least five balls so that he does not have to waste time chasing the balls.
6. After the snap the center should move down field simulating converging for the punt.

TYPE OF DRILL: Offensive
NAME OF DRILL: Leadership
TO BE USED BY: Centers
PURPOSE: To develop hustle and leadership qualities in the center
SET UP:

1. Centers pair off five yards "off" the ball.
2. One center acts as the quarterback and the other as the center.

3. The center has his back to the ball and the quarterback calls the snap count.

Instructions:

1. The quarterback calls the starting count and the players break for the line of scrimmage. The center gets set quickly and the quarterback calls the cadence. They both sprint five yards, place the ball on the ground and form a huddle five yards away from the ball and repeat the process.
2. If three centers are available, one of the centers becomes a dummy holder and the center will block him instead of sprinting five yards.
3. Players rotate so that they have a chance to be the center, the quarterback or the dummy holder.

Coaching points:

1. The center must hustle out of the huddle and get set quickly.
2. It is suggested that all drills start five yards from the ball so that the linemen get the idea of sprinting to the line. This develops sharpness plus being a good conditioner.

CHAPTER NINE

Winning Drills for in-Season Conditioning

This chapter pertains to that period in the practice session commonly called the conditioning period or as some coaches label it "the fourth quarter."

While most of the work accomplished during practice develops some form of physical conditioning this particular segment of practice has an emphasis on running.

The drills incorporated here not only deal with physical conditioning but also mental conditioning as well. It is also a time that is used to develop team discipline and second effort, teaching the squad members that the best conditioned team will make the best showing in the fourth quarter. A sense of pride is developed in that the players, knowing that when it comes down to the wire, they will win because they are in better condition than their opponents. The intensity of the conditioning period varies as the season progresses.

HIGH MORALE DRILLS

All the running in the world will not do any good unless the athlete has his "heart" in what he is doing, hence the drills used during this time should have high morale qualities and should never be used for punishment.

Competition either by the use of the stop-watch or by competing against one another enhances the close of practice drills.

COACH'S ATTITUDE

The attitude on the part of the coaching staff is very important during this period.

The coach should not confuse agility or reaction drills with conditioning drills. Obviously agility and reaction drills are used to develop agility and reaction and should not be used to a point where an athlete is so tired he cannot move. Agility and reaction drills should be short and are designed to accomplish a certain fundamental. Whereas conditioning drills are used to take the athlete as far as he can go, to show him that he had a little more than he thought he had. This gives the athlete a sense of accomplishment that he pushed himself to a point and did something that he had thought impossible.

INCORPORATE TEAM SKILLS WITH RUNNING

Running is the key to conditioning and this may be accomplished by incorporating some of the team skills such as punt coverage, punt return, kickoff coverage, kickoff return. By doing this the coach accomplishes two things at once which is important with the lack of practice time allotted.

Other times the coach may just want to use high morale type drills, such as sprints vs the clock or some of the various drills listed in this chapter. The coach accomplishes two things here also, physical as well as mental conditioning. At certain times during the season especially near the end of the campaign when a team lets up on the contact and the heavy work and there is a lot of running during the session then the conditioning period should be cut down or eliminated altogether.

A thought that the coach might want to think about is to "work them hard in victory and easy in defeat." Regardless of the drills used, the old adage still applies in that "The game should not be left on the practice field." If a team is not responding to the conditioning period and there does not seem to be a sense of pride developing the coach may want to look into the training rules because it is impossible to get a team in good condition if they do not have the discipline to follow the simple training rules. A well-conditioned team is disciplined not only on the field but off the field as well.

IN-SEASON CONDITIONING

Drill 1	Rabbit drill	To develop speed and second effort
Drill 2	Hare and Tortoise	To condition linemen while developing the second effort and desperation tackling
Drill 3	Ups and downs	To develop quickness in getting off the ground and to develop second effort
Drill 4	Giant drill	To develop high-knee action, balance and second effort during the conditioning period
Drill 5	Homer Beatty obstacle course	To develop balance, agility while working for conditioning
Drill 6	High stepper	To develop high-knee action and good lateral movement while conditioning
Drill 7	Northwestern running drill	To teach second effort while developing conditioning
Drill 8	Offside desire	To teach desire and second effort in downfield blocking while working on conditioning
Drill 9	Whistle drill	To develop second effort
Drill 10	Second effort drill	To teach second effort in blocking and tackling
Drill 11	Axt drill	To condition linemen while developing skills in the punting game

Drill 12	Punt coverage	To condition linemen while teaching the skills of good punt coverage
Drill 13	Punt return	To condition linemen while teaching the skills of a good punt return
Drill 14	Kickoff coverage	To condition linemen while teaching the skills of a proper kickoff coverage

TYPE OF DRILL: Conditioning
NAME OF DRILL: Rabbit
TO BE USED BY: Linemen
PURPOSE: To develop speed and second effort
SET UP:

1. Players line up on the goal line by positions, i.e. guards, tackles, centers.
2. One player, designated as the rabbit, steps out in front of the group. The distance the rabbit is out in front depends on his speed. Fast player takes about a five yard advantage and the slower player takes from ten to twenty yard advantage.

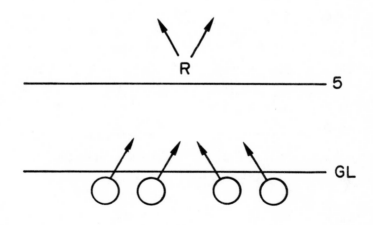

Diagram 9-1.

Instructions:

1. On the signal, all players start toward the opposite goal line with the idea of tagging the rabbit (Diagram 9-1).
2. The object is for all players to tag the rabbit. Conversely, the rabbit does not want to be tagged and will criss-cross down the field trying to stay away from the pack.

Coaching points:

1. The coach will make a game out of this and if the rabbit is tagged by all players some penalty must be imposed.
2. The players who do not tag the rabbit become the rabbit on succeeding turns.

TYPE OF DRILL: Conditioning
NAME OF DRILL: Hare-and-the-tortoise
TO BE USED BY: Linemen
PURPOSE: To condition linemen while developing the second effort and desperation tackling
SET UP:

1. Players line up on the goal line by positions, i.e. guards, tackles, centers.
2. One player is designated as the runner (hare) and one player is designated as the tackler (tortoise).

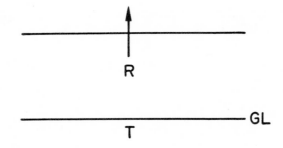

Diagram 9-2.

Instructions:

1. The runner takes a small lead (varies with speed) and on the signal they both start for the opposite goal line.

2. The tackler tries to make a desperation tackle from behind (Diagram 9-2).
3. If he makes the tackle, he gets off the runner and tries to get around in front of him before he starts out again.
4. The tackler continues to tackle the ball carrier, each time getting up, until they reach the opposite goal line.
5. The runner becomes the tackler on the way back.

Coaching points:

1. If the tackler does not make the tackle on the first try it then becomes a foot race to the other goal line, hence the runner should be placed in such a position that he will be tackled at least the first time.
2. Credit should be given for the number of tackles made during the drill.

TYPE OF DRILL: Conditioning
NAME OF DRILL: Ups-and-downs
TO BE USED BY: All linemen
PURPOSE: To develop quickness in getting off the ground and to develop second effort
SET UP:

1. On the command "Ready," the linemen assume a football position with their feet churning.
2. No particular formation is used for this as this drill can be performed at any time just where the players are standing.

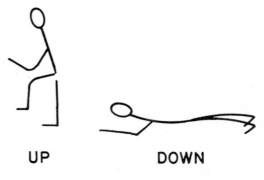

UP   DOWN

Diagram 9-3.

Instructions:

1. On command "Ready," players automatically assume a football position and begin to churn their feet.
2. On the command *down* they hit the ground in a prone position.
3. On command "Up" they assume the football position and churn their feet (Diagram 9-3).
4. This continues at the whim of the coach depending on his purpose at the time. If it is to shake the team if they are in a lackadaisical mood then just a few ups and downs are performed. If it is to see just what the football players are made of then the coach will continue. (The late Vince Lombardi was known to do 70 or 80 ups and downs at a time.)

Coaching points:

1. As stated above the coach must have a reason for doing this drill.

TYPE OF DRILL: Conditioning
NAME OF DRILL: Giant
TO BE USED BY: Lineman
PURPOSE: To develop high-knee action, balance and second effort during the conditioning period
SET UP:

1. Players line up on the goal line in single file by positions, guards, tackles, centers etc. Lines should be even in numbers.

Instructions:

1. On the signal from the coach, the first player sprints out five yards and assumes a prone position.
2. The next player jumps over the first player and assumes a prone position.
3. The rest of the players follow suit and after they have gone over the prone players assume the same position (Diagram 9-4).

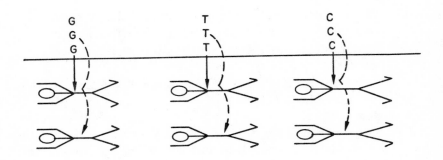

Diagram 9-4.

4. When the last man in line passes the first prone player, the prone player gets off the ground and goes down the line.
5. This continues until the first player in the line crosses the opposite goal line.

Coaching points:

1. Players should step over the buttock of the prone player to avoid any leg injuries.
2. The distance of the prone men must remain consistent.

TYPE OF DRILL: Conditioning
NAME OF DRILL: Homer Beatty obstacle course
TO BE USED BY: All Linemen
PURPOSE: To develop balance, agility while working for conditioning

SET UP:

1. This drill is run on the end line.
2. Players line up on the sideline. Three players hold dummies ten yards from the sideline, the goal posts are then used, then three dummies are placed on the ground ten yards from the goal posts and two dummies are held ten yards from the other sideline.

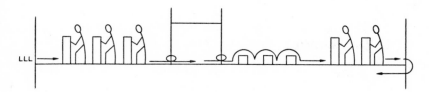

Diagram 9-5.

Instructions:

1. Players sprint to the first dummies, use a right, left, right shoulder block.
2. Players run around the first post with left hand on the ground, then around the second post with right hand on the ground.
3. Players high step over the dummies on the ground.
4. Players block the last two dummies, right and left shoulder, sprint to the sideline and circle back to the beginning of the drill (Diagram 9-5).

Coaching points:

1. After each obstacle players must regain balance simulating game type situations.

TYPE OF DRILL: Conditioning
NAME OF DRILL: High-stepper
TO BE USED BY: All Linemen
PURPOSE: To develop high knee action and good lateral movement

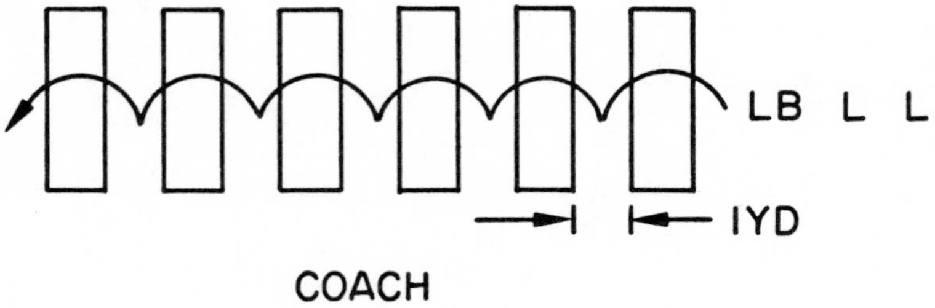

LB L L

⟶⊣ ⊢⟵ IYD

COACH

Diagram 9-6.

SET UP:

1. Dummies are placed on the ground, one yard apart.
2. The linemen line up parallel to the line of scrimmage.

Instructions:

1. Linemen face the dummies and run through with high-knee action.
2. Linemen face the coach and move laterally across the dummies with both feet touching the ground between dummies.
3. Linemen do a cross-over step across the dummies. Linemen start with a lead step and then the back foot hits the hole (Diagram 9-6).

Coaching points:

1. Coach should stress high-knee action on all maneuvers.
2. Coach should stress head up and good balance on all maneuvers.

TYPE OF DRILL: Conditioning
NAME OF DRILL: Northwestern-running
TO BE USED BY: Linemen
PURPOSE: To teach second effort while developing conditioning

SET UP:

1. Players line up by positions, i.e. guards, tackles, etc.
2. Players line up on the goal line facing the opposite goal line.
3. Players are numbered (Diagram 9-7).

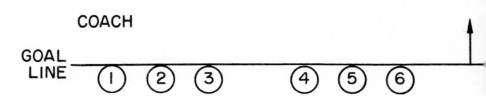

Diagram 9-7.

Instructions:

1. Players start down the field at ¾ speed. When they hit the 20-yard line the coach calls out a number.
2. All players begin to sprint toward the opposite goal line and the player whose number has been called will try to tag another one of the players.
3. There are two ways the drill can be run: 1—the player whose number has been called tries to tag as many players as possible or 2—once a player is tagged he then tries to tag someone else. He can tag the man who tagged him or go for someone else.
4. Once the players start their sprint they can run in any angle they desire in order to keep from being tagged.

Coaching points:

1. Players who have been tagged have to do push ups or some other activity.

TYPE OF DRILL: Conditioning
NAME OF DRILL: Offside-desire
TO BE USED BY: Linemen (need backfield for this drill)
PURPOSE: To teach desire and second effort in downfield blocking

SET UP:

1. A skeletal offense is set up, using a full backfield and the backside linemen. Dummies or markers are used to designate the on-side linemen.

Instructions:

1. The quarterback calls a play to the right (drill can be run both ways). Play action passes should also be thrown to keep the secondary honest (Diagram 9-8).
2. The offside or backside blockers or any player who has downfield responsibility (such as the flanker) are carefully checked on their hustle, condition and assignments.

Coaching points:

1. This is an unusual type of scrimmage in that the concentration is with the offside.

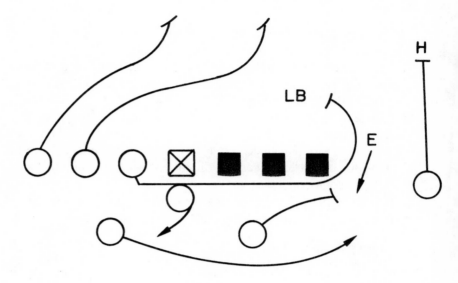

Diagram 9-8.

2. The defensive secondary may hold air dummies or shields so that the offside linemen will be able to carry out their assignments.

TYPE OF DRILL: Conditioning
NAME OF DRILL: Whistle
TO BE USED BY: Linemen and backs
PURPOSE: To develop second effort
SET UP:

1. Offensive and defensive teams.

Instructions:

1. This drill is a variation of a typical scrimmage (Diagram 9-9).
2. At the conclusion of each play, the coach blows a slow whistle, usually a six-second whistle.
3. Players carry out their assignments for six seconds regardless of whether the ball carrier is down or not. A blocker for example will continue his assignment until he hears the whistle.

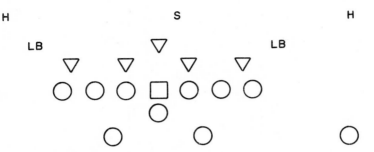

Diagram 9-9.

4. An added incentive that may be used is that the tackler cannot wrap his arms around the ball carrier. The tackler tries to knock the ball carrier down by use of a shoulder block.
5. Another variation is to delay the whistle, even longer than six seconds, to check on who is working and who is not.

Coaching points:

1. This is a hazardous drill and should be used only occasionally.

TYPE OF DRILL: Conditioning
NAME OF DRILL: Second-effort
TO BE USED BY: All Linemen
PURPOSE: To teach second effort in blocking and tackling

SET UP:

1. The drill is started with three offensive men and two defensive men. (Coach may use any combination, i.e. two on two, four on three etc.)
2. Mark off an area five yards wide and fifteen yards long.
3. Coaches and other players stand along boundaries.

Instructions:

1. Ball carrier and blockers start at the head of the chute and face the defensive men who may take any position they wish (Diagram 9-10).

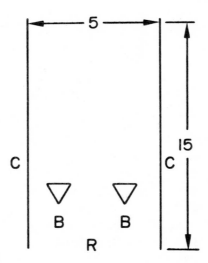

Diagram 9-10.

2. The object of the drill is to go down and back as fast as possible (stop-watch may be used).
3. The tacklers can tackle the ball carrier as many times as possible as long as he is moving.
4. The blockers block continually, even when the runner is down.
5. Tacklers must let the ball carrier up as quickly as possible so that he can continue up and back. The coach will blow a whistle when the ball carrier is down and blow it again when he is ready to run again.

Coaching points:

1. The coach must keep a close eye on this drill as it is aggressive and highly-spirited drill.
2. The rest of the squad members should be stationed along the side of the drill shouting encouragement.
3. The drill is very tiring and the coach should use good judgment on when and how long to use it.

TYPE OF DRILL: Conditioning

NAME OF DRILL: Axt Drill
TO BE USED BY: Linemen (punter necessary)
PURPOSE: To condition linemen while developing skills in the punting game
SET UP:

1. Set up a group of linemen and a punter. Competition between positions or offense vs defense enhances the drill.

Instructions:

1. One team will kick the ball from the twenty yard line and use proper punt coverage.
2. The receiving team will rush the punter and set up a punt return.
3. If backs are not used, the linemen may take turns receiving the ball. The rest of the team sets up one of the basic punt returns, i.e. wall right, wall left.
4. The covering linemen will use the proper techniques in covering the punt. If they are touched by one of the receiving team they will stop at that point to simulate being blocked.
5. The ball is dead where the ball carrier is tagged.
6. The receiving team now punts the ball and the punting team goes on defense.
7. This continues until one of the teams runs the ball back for a touchdown.

Coaching points:

1. This can be a live drill but it can become hazardous.

TYPE OF DRILL: Conditioning
NAME OF DRILL: Punt-coverage
TO BE USED BY: Linemen
PURPOSE: To condition linemen while teaching the skills of good punt coverage
SET UP:

1. Set up an offensive line, a punter and a safety man (Diagram 9-11).

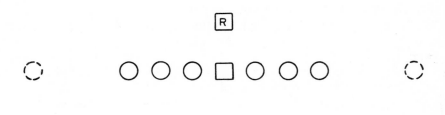

Diagram 9-11.

Instructions:

1. The ball is placed on the goal line with the punter standing in the end zone.
2. A tight punt is used in this case. The ball is kicked to the lone safety man and the linemen proceed down field in tight punt coverage.
3. A whistle may be blown at any time and all players will stop right where they are so that the coach may check the coverage. The whistle is blown again and the drill continues.
4. The punting team will line up at the point that the safety man was "downed."
5. The team lines up again and repeats the process. The coach may or may not blow the whistle.
6. Field position plays an important part in this drill in that certain types of formations are used and various types of kicks are used according to where the team is on the field.

TYPE OF DRILL: Conditioning
NAME OF DRILL: Punt-return
TO BE USED BY: Linemen
PURPOSE: To condition linemen while teaching the skills of a good punt return
SET UP:

1. Set up a defensive line, a safety man and a punter.

2. The coach may want to set up as the punter and throw the ball to save time. This eliminates the bad kicks and saves time on the drill.

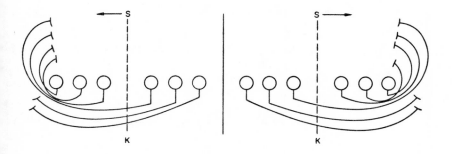

Diagram 9-12.

Instructions:

1. When the ball is punted (or thrown) the defensive linemen carry out their normal assignments (Diagram 9-12).
2. The coach may blow the whistle at any time and check the position of the linemen. He blows the whistle again and the drill continues.
3. The defensive men form a wall and then proceed to the goal line with the receiver.

Coaching points:

1. While the main purpose of this drill is to run, the coach is also using it to teach the proper method of setting the wall and escorting the ball carrier to the goal line.

TYPE OF DRILL: Conditioning
NAME OF DRILL: Kickoff-coverage
TO BE USED BY: Linemen
PURPOSE: To condition linemen while teaching the skills of proper kickoff coverage
SET UP:

1. Set up linemen in the proper kickoff formation.

2. Set up a kickoff man (coach may throw the ball) and a receiver.

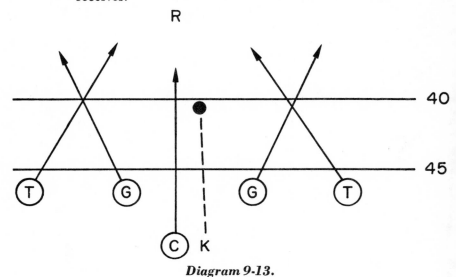

Diagram 9-13.

Instructions:

1. When the ball is kicked, the linemen who are positioned on the 40-yard line proceed down field covering the kickoff (Diagram 9-13).
2. The coach may blow a whistle at any time and the linemen will stop. The coach will check the routes and then blow the whistle again and the linemen will continue.
3. If the receiver out-runs the coverage, the linemen must pursue the ball carrier to the goal line.
4. Any type of coverage may be used, the one described above is just a sample.

Coaching points:

1. The whole kicking team may be used in this drill.
2. This is not only a good running drill to be used at the end of practice but teaches proper coverage techniques.

TYPE OF DRILL: Conditioning
NAME OF DRILL: Kickoff-return

TO BE USED BY: Linemen

PURPOSE: To condition linemen while teaching the skills of a proper kickoff return

SET UP:

1. Set up the linemen in the proper kickoff receiving formation.
2. Set up a place kicker (coach may throw the ball) and a safetyman.

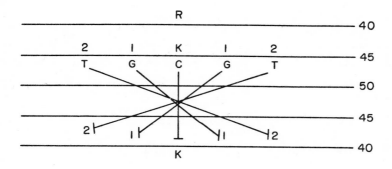

Diagram 9-14.

Instructions:

1. When the ball is kicked, the linemen will take their proper routes and escort the ball carrier to the goal line (Diagram 9-14).
2. The coach may blow the whistle at any time to check the routes of the linemen. The coach will blow the whistle again and linemen will proceed to the goal line.
3. The linemen jog back and the drill is repeated.
4. Any type of coverage may be used, the one described above is just a sample of a middle return.

Coaching points:

1. Linemen should be taught the proper rules about the kickoff game such as when the ball is live, when the ball is dead, etc.
2. The onside kickoff coverage should also be practiced.

TYPE OF DRILL: Conditioning
NAME OF DRILL: Signal-for-execution
TO BE USED BY: Linemen (whole team preferred)
PURPOSE: To condition a team while working for
                        proper execution in the running game
SET UP:

    1. Set up teams on the goal line. If three teams are used, place
    one in the middle of the field and one on each hash mark.

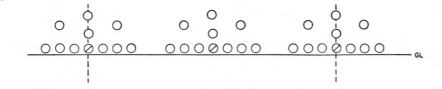

Diagram 9-15.

Instructions:

    1. The ball is placed on the goal line. The team breaks from a
    huddle and runs the play called for ten yards (Diagram
    9-15).
    2. The play must be perfectly executed. No fumble, no offside,
    etc.
    3. If the play is perfect, the ball is placed on the ten-yard line
    and the team returns to the huddle and the process is re-
    peated.
    4. The drill proceeds up the field stopping at each ten yard
    mark. If there is a mistake of any kind the team returns to
    the goal line and the drill is started over again.
    5. If more than one team is used, the drill may become com-
    petitive in that the first team to cross the other goal line
    wins.

Coaching points:

    1. The coach behind each team should insist on proper execu-
    tion.

TYPE OF DRILL: Conditioning

NAME OF DRILL: Signal-for-passing-execution
TO BE USED BY: Linemen, ends and quarterback
PURPOSE: To condition linemen while working on the passing game
SET UP:

1. Set up a skeletal offense, linemen, ends and a quarterback on the goal line. The whole team may be used in this drill if the coach so desires.
2. If more than one unit is to be used, the second and third units will line up behind the first unit and proceed with the drill once the first team has moved up field.

Instructions:

1. The quarterback calls a pass play in the huddle, the team breaks to the line and the play is called.
2. If the pass is complete, the receiver places the ball on the ground where the ball is caught. If it is caught near the sideline, the receiver will bring the ball to the nearest hash mark.
3. The linemen will run to where the ball has been caught and set up a huddle for the next pass play.
4. If the pass is incomplete, the team will return to the goal line and another pass will be called.
5. The object is to cross the opposite goal line.
6. The drill may be repeated as many times as the coach wishes.

TYPE OF DRILL: Conditioning
NAME OF DRILL: Flash-ball
TO BE USED BY: Linemen
PURPOSE: To condition linemen physically and mentally
SET UP:

1. Linemen "choose" teams of six to eight men each.
2. If the main field is available, three games may be played across the field otherwise any suitable area will do.

Instructions:

1. Flash ball is two-hand touch with the following rules:
   A. The offensive team gets three downs to make a touchdown.
   B. There is no huddle and there is no blocking.
   C. Each member of the defensive team takes a man and stays with him.
   D. There shall be only a one-man rush, i.e. the defensive man shall rush if his man is the quarterback.
   E. The quarterback may run or pass. The ball may be passed to any member of the team as many times as needed to score.
   F. The ball may be passed beyond the line of scrimmage either forward or backwards.
   G. If a pass is incomplete the ball will be "downed" from where the pass was thrown.

Coaching points:

1. The object of the game is to throw short passes (rugby style).
2. All offensive men should try to get open as they are all eligible to receive the ball.

CHAPTER TEN

Winning Drills for off-Season Conditioning

In this age of specialization the trend is to begin the next football season the day after the current football season ends. Football has become a twelve-month-a-year sport which all but eliminates the three-sport athlete. However, the high school football coach should encourage his athletes to participate in as many sports as possible. The off-season program for football should be for the boys that are not on other teams and should be sold on that premise.

There are varying points of view on the different types of off-season programs that are now being used. The following chapter deals with at least one drill in each of the following categories: Weight Training, Isometrics, Isotonics, Agilities, Flexibility Drills and Combative Activities. These programs are not a substitute for football but just to take up the slack between seasons with the idea of developing strength and speed.

On the plus side, these activities provide an opportunity for the athlete who is not participating in another sport to enhance his physical development rather than to stagnate between seasons.

The basic goal of the off-season program other than to develop strength, power and general physical conditioning for the season ahead, is to concentrate on certain parts of the body that will help the athlete become a better football player. The specifics would be: to develop strong arms and shoulders for tackling and blocking, to develop a strong back to help in absorbing the contact and lastly the knee and ankle muscles must be strengthened to avoid minor injuries. In addition to the above the athlete should develop flexibility and should improve endurance and running form.

There is a psychological feeling of well-being when the body is being developed to the fullest, the fat athlete who has turned this into muscle and speed, the small boy who has increased his weight and over-all stature.

All the while a sense of self-pride and team-pride is being developed which leads to the conclusion that the time spent in these various programs benefit the participant and the coach. As mentioned before we will just touch on a few of the basic off-season programs.

OFF-SEASON CONDITIONING PROGRAM

Drill 1	Pre-Season Routine	To build the body for the first days of football practice
Drill 2	Flexibility Drill	To develop body flexibility while getting ready for the season
Drill 3	Cal Stoll Flexibility Exercises	To develop flexibility
Drill 4	Quickness Builders	To develop good habits of quickness and agility
Drill 5	Wind Sprints	To improve endurance and running form
Drill 6	Combative Activities for Football Players	To develop aggressiveness, initiative, proper footwork and control of the body
Drill 7	Model Weight Program	To administer a systematic off-season weight program

Drill 8	Weight Training Program	To improve physical conditioning through strength, speed, endurance, power and agility
Drill 9	Chuck Coker PTA Program	High repetitions with heavy weights and minimum of rest
Drill 10	Isometric Program	To develop strength through static contraction
Drill 11	Isotonic Exercise	To build strength, develop endurance and increase flexibility.

TYPE OF DRILL: Pre-Season Warm-up training[1]
NAME OF DRILL: Pre-season-training-routine
TO BE USED BY: All Team Members
PURPOSE: To build the body for the first days of football practice

SET UP:

1. Athletes can do this on their own or get together with other team members.

Instructions: (Sample Chart)

August	8	9	10	11	12	13	14	15	16	17	18	19	20
Side Straddle Hop	20												50
Toe Toucher	20												30
Trunk Twister	15												30
Push Ups	25												50
Sit Ups	20												50
Neck Bridging	One minute									4 minutes			
1 Mile Run	1												4-5
Grass Drill	10												20
Forward Rolls	5												10

Complete the exercise period with any three exercises of your own.

---

[1] *Pre-Season Conditioning Manual,* American Football Coaches Association and the Tea Council of the USA, Inc.

Instructions:

Circle the number of repetitions according to the respective date (coach may insert number of reps). In addition the athlete should work on his particular skill: such as a guard pulling out of the line—left and right—also all should work on stance and starts—5 yds, 10 yds etc.

TYPE OF DRILL: Pre-Season practice[2]
NAME OF DRILL: Flexibility
TO BE USED BY: Linemen (whole team preferred)
PURPOSE: To develop body flexibility while getting ready for the season

SET UP:

1. Exercises may be done alone or with other teammates.

Instructions:

1. Stretching

Stretching exercises for leg, hip and lower back are a necessity for prevention of injury in these areas, especially the ham string. Flexibility in these muscles will increase the running stride.

2. Bounding

---

[2] *Ibid.*

Drum major strut, upper trunk leaning back as far as possible. Leg and arm action over-emphasized, used to improve knee action in running as well as stretching the thigh and hip joint muscles. Develops rhythm and exerciser should concentrate on relaxation.

3. Hip rotation

Develops a fuller range of hip rotation. Keep base foot flat on ground after becoming accustomed to the exercise. Swing leg in a smooth relaxed arc attempting to raise leg to maximum extension and height.

4. Form run against immobile object

Body should be at approximately 45-degree angle from fixed object. Knee concentrate on thigh being parallel to ground. Leg action should resemble piston-like motion. Improves body lean, knee lift, and leg drive. This exercise should be done at 5, 10 and 20 second bursts. Count the number of times one foot hits the ground during bursts to keep a record of improvement.

TYPE OF DRILL: Winter program
NAME OF DRILL: Cal Stoll flexibility exercises
TO BE USED BY: Linemen
PURPOSE: To develop flexibility
SET UP:

1. Linemen assemble in gym for workout. Program is broken down into three basic categories.
   A. Warm-up—Basic exercises, skipping rope, etc.
   B. Body isometrics—Players pair off and do a series of isometric exercises.
   C. Stretching (15 exercises):

   Number 1: On the back, feet together, locked up, bring feet up and touch them over the head to the floor, knees stiff.

   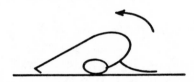

   Number 2: Spread the feet, spread the hands, without bending your knees, take the right foot and touch it to the left hand. Now take the left foot and touch it to the right hand.

   Number 3: Sitting position, feet spread, put chin on right knee then to the left one.

Number 4: Sitting position, feet spread, put chin on floor.

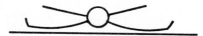

Number 5: Sitting position, feet together, chin down between the knees.

Number 6: Sitting position, take left knee and tuck it under chin, point toe at the sky, walk down your leg with your hands. Now the left one.

Number 7: Balance. Tuck both legs, make a V split. This is a V sit-up.

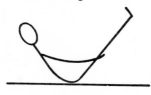

Number 8: Soles of feet tight together, bend knees out, akimbo. Pull soles in as tight as you can, take your elbows and push your knees down to the floor.

Number 9: Hurdler's stretch. Tuck the right foot, stretch out the left leg. Touch your chin to the left knee. Switch. Tuck the left foot, stretch out the right leg. Touch your chin to the right knee.

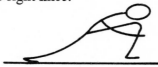

Number 10: Flat on your back, put your hands up over your head, palms flat on the floor. Get up on the toes, stretch, build a bridge. Stretch everything.

Number 11: Face your partner. Partner in a bent-over position. Put right leg up on back of partner. Back away, put chin on knee. Reverse procedure. Use left and right leg. Switch with partner.

Number 12: Put both feet together. Knees stiff, chin between your knees, walk down your legs with your hands.

Number 13: Front scaling. Put one leg behind you, hands out to the side, resting on one foot. Go for balance. Reverse.

Number 14: Standing, hands out, throw right leg up to the left hand, left leg to the right hand.

Number 15: Splits, sit down on the floor, legs out, try to put head to the floor.

TYPE OF DRILL: Pre-season conditioning
NAME OF DRILL: Quickness-builders
TO BE USED BY: Linemen (whole team preferred)
PURPOSE: To develop good habits of quickness and agility
SET UP:

1. Some of the drills may be done alone while others need a partner.

Instructions:

1. Rope skipping—Do this frequently. Skip for one to two minutes, rest, repeat.

2. Forward roll and sprint—Sprint ten yards, do a front somersault, come up running and repeat.
3. Jogging—Jog forward, backward, and sideward. Jog and break at a 45-degree angle. Jog and pivot.
4. Wave Drill (from standing position)—React to another man's movements, right, left, forward, backward.
5. Wave Drill (from a four-point position)—Do as the above only follow from a four-point stance.
6. Lateral Movement—Two men face each other with a line between them. On the starting count they race each other down the line sideways.
7. Snoop—Two men from a standing position attempt to grab the back of each other's knees. One point is scored for each time one of the contestants touches the other player behind the knee. Play game to five points.
8. Shadow Drill—Two men face one another in a five-yard area. One contestant uses evasive action to get past the other man without contact.
9. Over and Under—Two men, side by side, start in a four-point stance. The man on the right begins by going over the other man and finishes by assuming a four-point stance. The new man on the right begins by going under his partner. Alternate going under and over, and moving left and right.

Coaching points:

1. Speed in today's game is important in some instances but quickness is needed by all to keep up with the times.
2. Quickness and agility are the prime requisites needed to play modern football well.
3. Quickness off the ball both offensively and defensively are both required.

TYPE OF DRILL: Pre-season conditioning
NAME OF DRILL: Wind-sprints
TO BE USED BY: Linemen
PURPOSE: To improve endurance and running form
SET UP:

1. One or more athletes may participate.

Instructions:

1. Start with twenty-yard sprints, then progress to fifties, seventy-five yards and finally to one-hundred yards.
2. Some pointers on running form:
   A. The first step in sprinting is an explosive, hard-driving step, and more force is applied on each subsequent step.
   B. The toes are always straight ahead and knees are lifted high with the large muscles at the front of the thighs.
   C. Look for full-drive extension of the rear leg so that there is a straight line from the hip to the toe.
   D. Keep the shoulders square so that the arms do not rotate the shoulders or the hips.
   E. For relaxation, place the thumb over the forefinger. Tight fists slow you down.
   F. The arms are swung vigorously so that the hands come up as high as the chin and no further than the hips in the back swing.
   G. Breathing should be normal, inhaling and exhaling through the mouth.

TYPE OF DRILL: Winter program conditioning
NAME OF DRILL: Combative-activities
TO BE USED BY: Linemen
PURPOSE: To develop aggressiveness, initiative, proper footwork and control of body weight
SET UP:

1. Pair off players by size and weight.
2. The gym, wrestling room or any grass area will do.

Instructions:

1. The following are a group of combative exercises originally described by Robert J. Lynch of Rhode Island University:

   A. Wrestling to knock off feet

   The contestants face each other maneuvering to grasp their opponents in any manner in which they may knock their opponent off his feet, while still maintaining their own up-right position. The objective is to make your opponent touch the mat with any part of his body other than his hands or feet.

B. Stance drill

The contestants face each other in a three-point stance, using their free arm to push or pull their opponent off balance. They may circle each other or use any maneuver they wish as long as they maintain their three-point stance.

C. Stick wrestling

The contestants face each other, both holding a small stick (about as thick as a broom handle, two feet in length). You defeat your opponent by taking the stick away from him or by knocking him down.

D. Wrestling to lift off feet

The contestant maneuvers to grasp his opponent and to lift his body with both feet off the floor. You will soon discover that in order to make this particular lift, the boy must be in perfect tackling position. His knees must be bent, face on his opponent's chest, hand clasped under the buttock.

E. Back-to-back push

Two contestants stand back-to-back with elbows locked. Each contestant has right arm inside opponent's left arm. A base line is established ten feet in front of each contestant. At the starting signal, each, by pushing backwards, attempts to push the other over his base line. The contestants are not allowed to lift and carry their opponents. Only pushing is permitted.

F. Wrist bending

Opponents face each other, raise arms slightly upward and forward; lock fingers. The hands are brought downward between the contestants attempting to bend the wrists.

G. Back-to-back tug:

Same as the back-to-back pushing drill with the exception that each attempts to drag his opponent over the base line. Lifting and carrying is permitted.

H. Back-to-back, arms between legs

Each bends forward and extending his right arm between legs, grasps his opponent's right wrist. Pull him to the base line.

I. Hop and pull hands

Each man grasps his opponent's right hand, and hopping on his right foot, attempts to pull his opponent over the middle line. Either contestant loses automatically if he touches his rear foot to the ground. On successive bouts, they alternate hands and feet.

J. Step on toes

Each man attempts to step on the toes of his opponent. Time-limit—one minute.

K. Shoulder butt

Each man folds his arms across his chest and hops on right foot. He uses right shoulder and right side of chest to butt his opponent. The object is to make his opponent lose his balance and fall. To unfold his arms, or to touch his free foot to the ground means that he is disqualified.

L. Pull hands

The men grasp each others' wrists. At the starting signal, each man attempts to pull his opponent back across the base line. After a predetermined time, any player pulled across the middle line is also the loser. He must win three times in order to win the bout.

TYPE OF DRILL: Off-season weight training[3]

---

[3] *Off-season Weight Training Study,* Don W. Kloppenburg, Fresno City College, Fresno, California.

NAME OF DRILL: A-model-program
TO BE USED BY: Team members not involved in other sports
PURPOSE: To administer a systematic off-season weight program

SET UP:

1. Adjusted to local school facilities.

Instructions:

1. *Date of Program.* Preceding spring practice, February and March and preceding fall practice during the month of August. Monday, Wednesday and Friday devoted to lifting and Tuesday and Thursday devoted to not lifting activities (agility, balance, running, and fundamental skills).
2. *Time Allotment.* Administer weight-training for a time allotment ranging from 25–70 per cent of entire off-season football program. A planned one-hour program of lifting is suggested.
3. *Type of Lifting.* Administer a systematic type of lifting. Utilizing a combination of slow lift and quick explosive lift action, the type of lift for each exercise is based on the movement desired in the particular football skill.
4. *Exercise for Development of Football Skills*
    A. Blocking and Tackling. Military press, deep knee-bend toe raises, and bench press.
    B. Passing skill and power. Actual movement of passing with a weight in the hand. 20–30 repetitions.
    C. Ball carrying and defensive hand shiver. Arm curl, reverse arm curl and upright rowing.
5. *Exercises for Specific Body Development*
    A. Shoulder strength development. Military press.
    B. Arm-hand push-and-pull development. Arm curl and reverse arm curl.
    C. Back lift. Stiff and bent leg dead lift.
    D. Abdominal strength. Weighted sit ups and upright rowing.
    E. Lower body development. Deep knee-bend and toe raises.

TYPE OF DRILL: Off-season conditioning
NAME OF DRILL: Weight-training
TO BE USED BY: Linemen (whole team preferred)
PURPOSE: To improve physical conditioning through strength, speed, endurance, power and agility
SET UP:

1. Weight machine or barbells.
2. It is generally accepted that a three-a-week program is desirable for gaining strength and endurance. A schedule of workouts on alternate days is probably most practical. Those activities that require a great deal of running are especially desirable.
3. Speed of movement combined with strength or (force) is what causes a powerful action, and is exactly what you should condition yourself for in the execution of all exercises.
4. When following a three-a-week program, it has been found valuable to designate one day as a "heavy" day. On this day instead of attempting to increase your repetitions, add more weight and cut the repetitions by three or four. This method is sometimes called the reduction method.

5. *Terminology*

   A. Repetition: execution of an exercise from starting position back to the starting position (constitutes one repetition).
   B. Set: execution of an exercise a given number of repetitions. One set may consist of anywhere from 4–15 repetitions. A given exercise may be performed any number from 2–5 sets. A 2–3 minute rest between sets is recommended.
   C. Repetition maximum: the amount of weight that can be lifted a prescribed number of times. Usually exercises are performed in repetitions of 8, 10, or 15. One's repetition maximum then would be that amount of weight that could be exercised with 8 times, *not* 9, 10, or 11. It is this R.M. for each exercise that must be increased before any real gain in strength is achieved.

6. *List of Exercises.* The seven exercises that are considered as basic for all-around development are indicated by an asterisk:

Shoulders and arms

   *1. Over head press
   *2. Curl
    3. Arm elevation forward
    4. Arm elevation sideward
    5. Standing dumbbell press
    6. Triceps exercise
    7. Forearm curl
    8. Forearm wind
    9. Leaning lateral raise
   10. Wall weight-variation

Chest and arms

   *1. Bench press
    2. Pullovers
    3. Bench-lateral raise
    4. Inclined bench-dumbbell press
    5. Wall weight-variations

Upper back and neck

    1. Rowing
   *2. Upright rowing
    3. Shoulder shrug
    4. Neck raises
    5. Bridging
    6. Wall weight-variations

Lower back

   *1. Dead lift
    2. Trunk bender
    3. Back raises

Thighs and calves

   *1. Squat

2. Supine leg press
3. Leg curl
4. Vertical jump

Abdomen

*1. Sit-ups (45 sec. sets)
2. Table raise
3. Dumbbell-lateral bend
4. Wall weight variations

No particular order of exercise is given. However, certain factors are pointed out to the athletes.

1. The squat is perhaps the most exhaustive of any single exercise (plan accordingly).
2. Order of exercise should be varied from time to time for best efforts.
3. Light weight pullovers are good "spellers" between sets of squats on "heavy" days.
4. Lateral raises on the bench loosen tight biceps after curls.
5. Occasional substitution of different exercises for the same muscle groups makes for more interesting workouts.

POWER EXERCISES	PART EXERCISED	PRIMARY MUSCLES
two-arm curl	flexors	biceps
		brachialis
overhead press	abductors	deltoid
	flexors	coracobrachialis
	arm extensors	triceps
dead lift, straight	back extensors	sacraspinalis
legs	hip extensors	gluteus maxims
sit up	flexors	rectus abdomnis
	hip flexors	obliques
		psoas major
neck flexion &	flexors	sternomastoid
extensions	extensors	scaleni muscles
		prevertebral muscles
		sacrospinalis
		splenius

squat	thigh extensors	deep posterior spinal gluteus maxims quadriceps
	lower leg extensors	
bench press	shoulder horizontal	anterior deltoid
	flexors	pectoralis major
	arm extensors	triceps
rowing	extensors	latissimus dorsi
	arm flexors	tres major
		brachialis

TYPE OF DRILL:	Off-season weight program
NAME OF DRILL:	*Chuck-Coker-PTA-program
TO BE USED BY:	Linemen (whole team preferred)
PURPOSE:	The Pain, Torture and Agony program uses high repetitions with heavy weights and minimum of rest
SET UP:	A weight machine is desirable

Instructions:

1. This program should only be used after the athlete has had several months of basic weight training.
2. Program
   A. Leg press. 1 set, all you can do with 60% maximum weight.
   B. Bench press. 1 set, same as above.
   C. Calf exercise. 1 set, same as above.
   D. Lat pull-down. 1 set front, 1 set back, same as above.
   E. Squat clean (bench press station) 1 set, same as above.

Coaching points:

1. Example: A lineman charges approximately 100 times a game. He should set his maximum goal to: 100 leg presses with double his body weight.
2. It takes some time for the high levels of repetitions to be reached. When sufficient stamina has been developed the athlete will be able to stand the stress of Pain, Torture and Agony.

---

* Chuck Coker. President of Universal Athletic Sales

This program will produce: pain tolerance, improved stamina and endurance, confidence, competition stress and all around physical toughness.

TYPE OF DRILL: Pre-Season Conditioning
NAME OF DRILL: Isometric-program
TO BE USED BY: Linemen
PURPOSE: To develop strength through static contraction

SET UP:

1. Set up a power rack. Two 2′ x 6′s set in cement about eight feet high. Drill holes about two and a half inches apart and they should be off center. A piece of inch and a half pipe will do for the bar (Diagram 10-1).

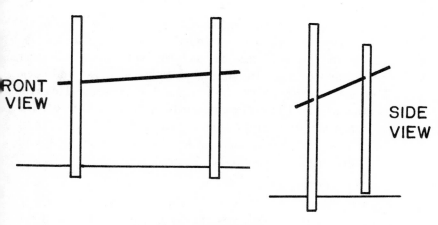

Diagram 10-1.

Instructions: basic exercises

1. THE WARM-UP LEG LIFT
   Hang from the bar for several seconds. While hanging, raise the knees up to the chest. Repeat this several times.

   Note: The following exercises should start with a period of six seconds. Add two seconds a week until you reach twelve seconds.

2. DEAD LIFT

Place the bar just below knee level. Face the bar with the knees bent slightly. Feet should be shoulder width apart with the insteps directly under the bar. Place the hands on the bar, knuckles out and pull for allotted time. This exercise will develop the muscles of the lower back and the muscles across the back of the shoulders.

3. SHOULDER SHRUG

This exercise is performed by standing up straight, with the bar at a height where it will be handy when your arms are fully extended downward. Grip the bar with the hands close together. Shrug the shoulders upward as hard as possible. This exercise develops the muscles of the shoulders and upper portion of the big trapezius muscles of the back and neck.

4. HIGH PRESS

Set the bar about four inches below the height of the hands when the arms are fully extended overhead. Stand directly under the bar, grasp the bar with the hands about shoulder width apart. Look straight ahead, tighten leg, hip and back muscles and push on the bar as hard as possible. This is a good exercise to develop the pushing muscles on the back of the arms, shoulder and the neck muscles. The muscles of the back, abdominal wall and legs are also developed with this exercise.

5. LEG CURL

This exercise is performed by lying in a prone position on a bench with the knees extending just over the end of the bench. The bench is in front of the bar and the bar is placed just high enough to hook the heel under it. Try to bend the knees with the heels locked under the bar. There are three positions: low, legs nearly fully extended; mdium, legs three quarters of the way up; and high, legs bent at right angles to the body.

6. RISE ON TOES

This exercise is performed with the bar about two inches above knee height. The athlete sits on the bench so that his knees are directly under the bar and his feet are directly under his knees. His lower leg should be perpendicular to the ground. He should use a pad of some type between his knees and the bar. After he is in position, he should raise his heels off the ground and force his knees up against the bar. This exercise should be done with the toes straight, again with the toes pointed out. This exercise will develop the explosive power needed in starting and running.

7. LEG PRESS

This exercise can be performed either from a bench or from lying on the ground. The athlete lies on his back with his hips directly under the bar and his feet up against the bar. At the start of this exercise the angle of the knees should be about 150 degrees. The pelvis should be flat on the ground and the head should be held up off the ground, with the chin near the chest. This is a good exercise for developing maximum leg strength and power, also for the prevention of knee injuries.

8. BENCH PRESS

Now bring the bench up and place it between the uprights and place the bar about four inches above the chest and press as hard as you can for the start of the bench press. The bar should be moved up another three inches and press again.

9. CURLS

Grasp the bar with the palms up. Carry out the action as described for upright rowing. Pull as hard as you can with your arm for six seconds. Start with the bar at a position waist high. You may move the bar up or down for more specialized action.

TYPE OF DRILL: Off-season conditioning
NAME OF DRILL: Isotonic-exercise
TO BE USED BY: Linemen (whole team preferred)
PURPOSE: To build strength, develop endurance and increase flexibility

SET UP:

1. The use of an Exer-Genie exerciser is required.

Instructions:

1. Set the Exer-Genie exerciser at resistance you wish to use.
2. Exercise should be started with a 10 second isometric contraction. Apply sufficient pressure, push, or pull on the trail line so that you cannot move the line through the exerciser. Pull or push as hard as you can for ten seconds.
3. Now, without hesitating for even a moment, release the pressure on the trail line partially or completely as exercise dictates and move through the full range of motion.
4. For general physical conditioning do the "Big Four" three times. Pause a minute or two between each repetition, or until your breathing becomes normal and your pulse rate drops to approximately 120.
5. The Big Four consists of: Ten second isometric hold, dead left, leg press, curl or upright row and military press, as a continuous exercise, without pause. Entire exercise should take about twenty-two seconds.
6. The Exer-Genie makes it possible to isolate specific muscle groups. Exercises which are particularly effective for various parts of the body are:

Body Area	*Exercises*
Abdomen, Mid-section and Lower back	Sit up, Forward Bend, Rowing
Side	Side Bend
Chest	Chest
Upper body	Lats Pulley, Rowing Standing Bench Press
Neck	Neck
Arms	Triceps Pull, Curl
Legs and hips	Bicycle, Thigh Pulls

Note: Normally three repetitions of the selected exercise are recommended.

7. *Ten Station Circuit*

The ten station circuit is a coordinated sequence of exercises designed to provide maximum conditioning and training benefits through the principle of pre-set resistance. Three Big Four stations are spaced throughout the circuit, so that the major muscles of the body are worked isometrically and isotonically. Other stations are designed to exercise specific muscles through a full range of motion at capacity resistance while the antagonistic muscles are completely relaxed. This helps to produce a notable increase in the flexibility of the muscles exercised.

Station 1. Big Four
Station 2. Lats Pulley
Station 3. Bench Press
Station 4. Triceps Pull
Station 5. Big Four
Station 6. Rowing
Station 7. Sit Up
Station 8. Bicycle
Station 9. Big Four
Station 10. Running

Two athletes can occupy a station. It is possible to work out as many as twenty at any given moment. A workout can be completed, all boys having exercised at each of the stations in about ten minutes.

Note: Instruction manuals for the Exer-Genie exerciser may be obtained from Dean Miller, Exer-Genie, Inc., P.O. Box 3237, Fullerton, California 92634.

Index

A

Abe Martin drill, 181–182
Across-the-bow drill, 91–92
    for defensive linemen, 142–143
Aggressiveness essential for good tack-
    ling, 172
Agility and warm-up drills, 29–55
    calisthenics as means of organiza-
        tion, 30, 31
    running, combining with, 30–32
    master plan, 29–30
    pre-practice work, 32–55
        Barrel-Run, 39–40
        Carrioca, 42–43
        chart, 32–33
        Dummy-Crab, 38–39
        Explosion, 46–47
        Hurdle-Steps, 37–38
        Hurdlers-Stretch, 41–42
        Indiana-stripes, 33–34
        Indiana-touch, 54–55
        Mirror, 53–54
        Modified-quarter-eagle, 44–45
        Monkey-crawl, 34–35
        Monkey-Roll, 47–48
        Prone-running, 45–46
        Quick-Calls, 35–36
        Relay-jack, 51–52
        Scramble, 43–44
        Shuffle-Seat-roll, 48–50
        Square, 36–37

        Stretching, 40–41
        Supine-running, 50–51
        360-Degree-fumble, 55
        Wave, 52–53
    time and place for, 29
Alternating drill for centers, 236–237
American Football Coaches Associa-
    tion, 269n
Angle-tackling drill, 177–178
Arm-and-wrist-strength drill, 241
Around-the-circle drill, 79–80
Around-the-hat drill, 113–114
Attitude of coach during in-season
    drills, 246
Axt drill, 259

B

Back-to-back push, 278
Back-to-back tug, 279
    arms between legs, 279
Bad-ball drill, 223–224
Ball carrier: locating, importance of to
    defensive lineman, 128
    pursuit of by defensive lineman, 128
Barrel-Run drill, 39–40
Beatty-armless-tackling drill, 196–197
"Big Four" in isotonic exercises, 288
Billy-goat drill, 206–207
Block protection drill, 159–162
    Dip charge technique, 162
    Hand shiver technique, 161

Block protection drill (*cont.*)
    Loop charge, 162
    Low shoulder and forearm charge, 160
    Rip up and lift, 160–161
    Slant charge technique, 161–162
Blocking, drills for, 57–105 (see also "Linemen, blocking, winning drills for")
Blocking-a-stunting-defense drill, 103–105
Board drill, 66–67
    for defensive linemen, 163–164
Bryant, Bear, 21
Buckley-wall drill, 168–169
Bull-in-the-ring drill, 202–203
Burma-road drill, 82–83

C

Cal Stoll flexibility exercises, 272–275
Calisthenics as means of organization, 30, 31
    running, combining with, 30–32
Call drill, 111–112
Carrioca drill, 42–43
Cat-and-mouse drill, 188–189
Catching-in-a-crowd drill, 226–227
Center, drills for, 231–244
    Alternating drill, 236–237
    Arm-and-wrist-strength drill, 241
    Center-quarterback-exchange drill, 234–235
    Center-warm-up drill, 232–233
    Center's-stance drill, 233–234
    Centering-for-the-punt drill, 240–241
    Exchange-drill-vs-sled drill, 235–236
    Fundamentals-of-blocking drill, 238–239
    as most important position on offensive line, 230
    Leadership drill, 243–244
    Speed-and-snap drill, 241–242
    Stance-warm-up drill, 233
    Tire drill, 242–243
    Wrist-snap drill, 239–240
Center-quarterback-exchange drill, 234–235
Center-warm-up drill, 232–233
Center's-stance drill, 233–234
Centering-for-the-punt drill, 240–241
Chart, master, 21–22, 23
Chase of ball carrier essential to defensive play, 128
Chuck-Coker-PTA-program, 284–285
Chute-get-off drill, 77–78

Cluster drill for defensive linemen, 135–136
Coach's attitude during in-season drills, 246
Coach's enthusiasm as key factor in success of drill, 26
Coker, Chuck, 284, 284*n*
Combative activities as drills, 277–279
Combination drill, 75–76
    5-on-5, 117
Competitive drills as best type, 26
Conditioning, in-season, drills for, 245–266 (see also "In-season conditioning . . .")
    off-season, drills for, 267–289 (see also "Off-season conditioning . . .")
Confidence tackling drill, 173–174
Correct-step drill, 108
Cross-body-block drill, 62–63
Cross drill, 114–115

D

Daugherty, Duffy, 21
Defensive line, drills for, 127–170
    Across-the-bow drill, 142–143
    ball carrier, locating, 128
    ball carrier, pursuing, 128
    Block-protection, 159–162
        Dip charge technique, 162
        hand shiver, 161
        Loop charge, 162
        Low shoulder and forearm charge, 160
        Rip up and lift, 160–161
        Slant charge, 161–162
    Board, 163–164
    Buckley-wall drill, 168–169
    Cluster drill, 136
    Eagle drill, 131–132
    5-on-2 drill, 141–142
    Forearm-Lift-Technique drill, 132–133
    Forearm-lift-on-sled, 149–150
    Forearm-shiver-on-the-sled drill, 148
    gang tackling, 128
    Get-to-them drill, 164–165
    going around blocker, 128
    Hit-pivot-and-pursue drill, 154–155
    Hit-pivot-and-shed-vs-the-sled drill, 158–159
    Hit-and-pursue-vs-the-sled drill, 153–154
    Hit-and-rush-vs-the-sled drill, 165–166

Defensive line (*cont.*)
  Hit-shed-pursue-and-tackle drill, 143–144
  Mazzucca-speed drill, 169–170
  moving on ball, 127
  neutralizing offensive charge, 128
  one-on-one-fumble-recovery, 152–153
  Pass-rush-vs-2-man-Sled vs Sprint and Roll-out Passer drill, 166–168
  protecting territory, 128
  Pursuit-and-chase drill, 145–146
  Reacting-to-the-Sweeps or Pass, 162–163
  Reaction drill, 133–134
  Seat-roll-vs-the-sled drill, 147–148
  Shed-the-blocker-and-pursue-vs-the-sled drill, 157–158
  Shed-and-shuffle drill, 144–145
  Shooting-the-gap drill, 137
  Spin-out-vs-the-seven-man-sled drill, 150–151
  Splitting-the-seam drill, 139–140
  Stance drill, 128–130
  Step drill, 130–131
  striking blow, 128
  Ten-twenty drill, 156–157
  Three-on-one drill, 151–152
  Two-on-one drill, 140–141
  West Point drill, 138–139
  Whirl-out-vs-the-sled drill, 155–156
Determination essential for good tackling, 172
Dip charge technique of block protection, 162
Disengaging offensive blocker, importance of for defensive lineman, 128
Downfield-recognition drill, 81–82
Drill chart, master, 21–22, 23
  daily, 22, 23–24
Drills, four types of, 19
Drop-back-pass-protection drill, 95–97
Dummy-Crab drill, 38–39
Dummy-dropper drill, 213–215

E

Eagle drill, 131–132
Early drills, 32–55
  chart, 32–33
Emotional "keying-up" for tackling, 172
Enthusiasm of coach as key factor to success of drill, 26
Equipment, setting up before drill, 26
Exchange-drill-vs-sled drill, 235–236
Exer-Genie exerciser, 288–289

Explosion drill, 46–47
  for linemen, 86–87
Explosive form tackling drill, 179–180
Eye-opener drill, 230

F

Find-the-backer drill, 80–81
5-on-2 drill, 141–142
Flash-ball drill, 265–266
Flexibility drill, 270–271
Forearm-lift-on-sled drill, 149–150
Forearm-Lift-Technique drill, 132–133
Forearm-shiver-on-the-sled drill, 148
Form-block-on-the-two-man-sled drill, 89–90
Form-explosion drill, 184–185
Form-tackling-vs-the-sled drill, 192–193
Formula for coaching linemen, 19
"Fourth quarter" conditioning, drills for, 245–266
  (see also "In-season conditioning . . .")
Fresno City College, 280n
Fumble-drill-and-reaction drill, 227–228
Fundamentals-of-blocking drill for centers, 238–239
Fundamentals-of-pass-blocking drill, 97–98
Funnel drill, 112–113

G

Gang tackling, 128
Get-to-them drill, 164–165
Giant drill, 251–252
Goal line, running toward in drills, 27
Goal-line-tackling, 185–186
Guard-reaction drill, 215–217
Guarding-the-line drill, 115–117

H

Half-bull drill, 201–202
Hand-and-eye-coordination drill, 221–222
Hand shiver technique of block protection, 161
Hare-and-the-tortoise drill, 249–250
Harmony, staff, essential for successful drills, 24
High morale drills, 246
High-stepper drill, 253–254
Hints for successful drills, 24–27
"Hit or get hit" basic philosophy of drills, 25

Hit-and-hunt vs the two-man sled drill, 194–195
Hit-pivot-and-pursue drill, 154–155
Hit-pivot-and-shed-vs-the-sled drill, 158–159
Hit-and-pursue-vs-the-sled drill, 153–154
Hit-and-recoil drill, 88–89
Hit-and-rush-vs-the-sled drill, 165–166
Hit-shed-pursue-and-tackle drill, 143–144
Hit-shuffle-and-tackle vs the sled drill, 191–192
Homer Beatty obstacle course, 252–253
Hop and pull hands, 279
Huddle, starting drills from, 25
Hurdle-Steps drill, 37–38
Hurdlers-Stretch drill, 41–42

I

In-season conditioning, drills for, 245–266
    Axt drill, 259
    coach's attitude, 246
    Flash-bar drill, 265–266
    Giant drill, 251–252
    Hare-and-the-tortoise drill, 249–250
    high morale drills, 246
    High-stepper drill, 253–254
    Homer Beatty obstacle course drill, 252–253
    Kickoff-coverage drill, 261–262
    Kickoff-return drill, 262–263
    Northwestern-running drill, 254–255
    Offside-desire drill, 255–256
    Punt-coverage drill, 259–260
    Punt-return drill, 260–261
    purposes of drills, 247–248
    Rabbit drill, 248–249
    running, incorporating team skills with, 246–247
    Second-effort drill, 257–258
    Signal-for-execution drill, 264
    Signal-for-passing-execution drill, 265
    Ups-and-downs drill, 250–251
    Whistle drill, 256–257
Indiana-circle drill, 68–69
Indiana-stripes drill, 33–34
Indiana-touch drill, 54–55
Isometric program, 285–287
Isotonic exercise drills, 287–289

K

Keying drill for linebackers, 199–200
Kickoff-coverage drill, 261–262

Kickoff-return drill, 262–263
King-of-the-cage drill, 78–79
Kloppenburg, Don W., 280*n*

L

Lateral-movement drill, 225–226
Lead-blocking drill, 71
Leadership drill, 243–244
Leverage drill, 65–66
Line-marking for drills, 26–27
Linebacker-one-on-one drill, 211–212
Linebacker-three-on-one drill, 215
Linebackers, drills for, 199–230
    Bad-ball drill, 223–224
    Billy-goat drill, 206–207
    Bull-in-the-ring drill, 202–203
    Catching-in-a-crowd drill, 226–227
    Dummy-dropper drill, 213–215
    Eye-opener drill, 230
    Fumble-drill-and-reaction drill, 227–228
    Guard-reaction drill, 215–217
    Half-bull drill, 201–202
    Hand-and-eye-coordination drill, 221–222
    Keying drill, 199–200
    Lateral-movement drill, 225–226
    Linebacker-one-on-one drill, 211–212
    Linebacker-three-on-one drill, 215
    Little-bull drill, 209–210
    Mazzucco-bump drill, 209
    Mirror drill, 204–205
    My-ball drill, 217–218
    Roll-and-hit drill, 203–204
    Running-the-line drill, 228–229
    Scramble-drill vs the sled, 205–206
    Scrape drill, 207–208
    Shed-and-tackle drill, 212–213
    Tennessee-backer drill, 219–220
    Tennessee-shadow drill, 210–211
    Through-a-man-to-the-ball drill, 222–223
    Tip drill, 220–221
    Twenty-catch drill, 218–219
    Zone coverage drill, 224–225
Linemen, blocking, winning drills for, 57–105
    Across-the-bow drill, 91–92
    Around-the-circle drill, 79–80
    Blocking-a-stunting-defense drill, 103–105
    Board drill, 66–67
    Burma-road drill, 82–83
    Chute-get-off drill, 77–78
    Combination drill, 75–76
    Cross-body-block drill, 62–63

Linemen blocking (*cont.*)
  Downfield-recognition drill, 81–82
  Drop-back-pass-protection drill, 95–97
  Explosion drill, 86–87
  Find-the-backer drill, 80–81
  Form-block-on-the-two-man-sled, 89–90
  Fundamentals-of-pass-blocking drill, 97–98
  Hit-and-recoil drill, 88–89
  Indiana-circle drill, 68–69
  King-of-the-cage drill, 78–79
  Lead-blocking drill, 71
  Leverage drill, 65–66
  Lovers-lane drill, 94–95
  McQueary-blitz-blocking drill, 101–102
  McQueary-screen-pass drill, 102–103
  Musical-dummies drill, 83–84
  Near-foot-near-shoulder drill, 61–62
  Offensive-get-off-vs-the-sled, 87–88
  Piedmont-pad drill, 92–93
  position or stance, 58
  Post-block drill, 70
  Post-and-lead drill, 72–73
  Post-lead-and-slide drill, 73–74
  Progression-pass-protection drill, 99–101
  Push-and-pull drill, 93–94
  Reach-and-scramble drill, 63–64
  React-and-hunt drill, 90–91
  Reverse-body-block drill, 60–61
  Reverse-shoulder-block-to-a-crab drill, 59–60
  Root-hog drill, 67–68
  Shoulder-block drill, 58–59
  Shoulder-block-vs-the-Red-Monster, 74–75
  Six-on-six drill, 76–77, 98–99
  Sled-progression drill, 84–85
  Step-jolt drill, 64–65
Little-bull drill, 209–210
Lombardi, Vince, 57, 251
Loop charge technique of block protection, 162
Lovers-lane drill, 94–95
Low shoulder and forearm charge of block protection, 160
Lynch, Robert J., 277

M

Marked areas for drills, 26–27
Master drill chart, 21–22, 23
Master plan for warm-up drills, 29–30

Mazzucco-speed drill, 169–170
Mazzucco-bump drill, 209
McQueary-blitz-blocking drill, 101–102
McQueary-screen-pass drill, 102–103
Miller, Dean, 289
Mirror drill, 53–54
  for linebackers, 204–205
Model-program for off-season conditioning, 280
Modified-quarter-eagle drill, 44–45
Monkey-crawl drill, 34–35
Monkey-Roll drill, 47–48
Morale drills, 246
Moving on ball, importance of for defensive lineman, 127
Musical-dummies drill, 83–84
My-ball drill, 217–218

N

Naming drills, importance of, 25
Near-foot-near-shoulder drill, 61–62
Neutralizing offensive blow, importance of for defensive lineman, 128
Northwestern-running drill, 254–255

O

Obstacle-tackling drill, 189–190
Off-season conditioning, drills for, 267–289
  Cal Stoll flexibility exercises, 272–275
  Chuck-Coker-PTA-program, 284–285
  Combative-activities, 277–279
  Flexibility drill, 270–271
  Isometric program, 285–287
  Isotonic exercise drills, 287–289
  model program, 280
  pre-season-training-routine, 269–270
  purposes of, 268–269
  Quickness-builders drill, 275–276
  weight-training, 281–284
  Wind-sprints, 276–277
Off-season Weight Training Study, 280n
Offensive-get-off-vs-the-sled drill, 87–88
Offside-desire drill, 255–256
Oklahoma-tackling drill, 187
One-on-one fumble-recovery drill, 152–153
1–2–3 Trap, 109–110
Organizing and coaching winning line drills, 19–27
  daily drill chart for linemen, 22, 23–24
  drills, four types of, 19

Organizing and coaching winning line
    drills (*cont.*)
  formula, 19
  hints for successful drills, 24–27
  master drill chart, 21–22
  plan your time and time your plan,
    20–21
  suggestions for, 21
Over-doing a drill, 26

P

Pass-rush-vs-2-man-Sled vs Sprint-and
    Rollout Passer drill, 166–168
Piedmont-pad drill, 92–93
Planning your time, 20–21
Post-block drill, 70
Post-and-lead drill, 72–73
Post-lead-and-slide drill, 73–74
Pre-practice drills, 32–55
  chart, 32–33
Pre-season Conditional Manual, 269n
Pre-season training routine, 269–270
Progression-pass-protection drill,
    99–101
Prone-running drill, 45–46
Protecting territory as first obligation
    of defensive lineman, 128
Pull-and-cut drill, 123–124
Pull hands, 279
Pull-and-seal drill, 118–119
Pulling and trapping linemen, drills
    for, 107–125
  Around-the-hat drill, 113–114
  Call, 111–112
  Combination drill—5-on-5, 117
  Correct-step drill, 108
  Cross drill, 114–115
  Funnel drill, 112–113
  Guarding-the-line, 115–117
  1–2–3 Trap, 109–110
  Pull-and-cut-drill, 123–124
  Pull-and-seal, 118–119
  Quick-pitch, 119–120
  Sweep, 121–122
  3-on-3 Trap, 120–121
  Trap-vs-Stunts, 122–123
  Trapping-the-board, 110–111
  Trapping-the-Two-Man-Sled drill,
    125
Punt-coverage drill, 259–260
Punt-return drill, 260–261
Pursuit of ball carrier essential to defen-
    sive play, 128
Pursuit-and-chase drill, 145–146
Push-and-pull drill, 93–94

Q

Quick-Calls drill, 35–36
Quick-pitch drill, 119–120
Quickness-builders drill, 275–276

R

Rabbit drill, 248–249
Reach-and-scramble drill, 63–64
React-and-hunt drill, 90–91
Reacting-to-the-Sweeps-or-Pass drill,
    162–163
Reaction drill for defensive linemen,
    133–134
Reduction method in weight-training,
    281
Relay-jack drill, 51–52
Reverse-body-block drill, 60–61
Reverse-shoulder-block-to-a-crab drill,
    59–60
Rhode Island University, 277
Rhythm-reaction and Tackle drill, 175–
    176
Rip up and lift technique of block pro-
    tection, 160–161
Roll-and-hit drill for linebackers, 203–
    204
Roll-and-tackle drill, 178–179
Root-hog drill, 67–68
Running, combining with calisthenics,
    30–32
  importance of in drills, 25–26
  incorporating team skills with, 246–
    247
Running-the-line drill, 228–229

S

Scramble drill, 43–44
Scramble-drill vs the sled drill, 205–
    206
Scrape drill, 207–208
Seat-roll-vs-the-sled drill, 147–148
Seat-roll-and-tackle vs the sled drill,
    193–194
Second-effort drill, 257–258
Shed-the-blocker-and-pursue-vs-the-sled
    drill, 157–158
Shed-and-shuffle drill, 144–145
Shed-and-tackle drill, 212–213
Shooting-the-gap drill, 137
Shoulder-block drill, 58–59
Shoulder-block-vs-the-Red-Monster
    drill, 74–75
Shoulder butt, 279

Shuffle-Seat-roll drill, 48–50
Sideline tackling drill, 180–181
Signal-for-execution drill, 264
Signal-for-passing-execution drill, 265
Simplicity as key word in football, 127
Six-on-six drill, 76–77
    for linemen, 98–99
Slant charge technique of block protec-
    tion, 161–162
Sled-progression drill, 84–85
Speed-and-snap drill, 241–242
Spin-out-vs-the-seven-man-sled drill,
    150–151
Splitting-the-seam drill, 139–140
Square drill, 36–37
Square-tackling drill, 195–196
Stance, correct, essential for successful
    drills, 24
Stance drill, 278
    for defensive linemen, 128–130
Stance-warm-up drill for centers, 233
Starting count, using to start drill, 26
Step drill for defensive linemen, 130–
    131
Step-jolt drill, 64–65
Step on toes, 279
Stick wrestling, 278
Stretching drill, 40–41
"Stripes," 30–32
Suggestions for drill organization, 21
Supine-running drill, 50–51
Sweep drill, 121–122

T

Tackling linemen, drills for, 171–197
    Abe Martin drill, 181–182
    Angle-tackling, 177–178
    Beatty-armless tackling drill, 196–197
    Cat-and-mouse drill, 188–189
    Confidence tackling drill, 173–174
    emotional keying-up, 172
    Explosive form tackling, 179–180
    factors, basic, 172
    Form-explosion drill, 184–185
    Form-tackling vs the sled drill, 192–
    193
    Goal-line-tackling drill, 185–186
    Hit-and-hunt vs the two-man sled
    drill, 194–195
    Hit-shuffle-and-tackle vs the sled drill,
    191–192
    Obstacle-tackling drill, 189–190
    Oklahoma-tackling drill, 187
    Rhythm-reaction and Tackle drill,
    175–176
    Roll-and-tackle drill, 178–179
    Seat-roll-and-tackle vs the sled drill,
    193–194
    Sideline tackling, 180–181
    Square-tackling drill, 195–196
    Tackling-vs-the-two-man-sled, 190–
    191
    Through-a-blocker drill, 183–184
    Through-a-man drill, 176–177
    Triangle drill, 182–183
    Walk-through Tackling drill, 172–173
Tackling-vs-the-two-man-sled drill, 190–
    191
Tea Council of the USA, Inc., 269n
Ten-twenty drill, 156–157
Tennessee-backer drill, 219–220
Tennessee-shadow drill, 210–211
Territory, protection of as first obli-
    gation of defensive lineman, 128
Three-on-one drill for defensive line-
    men, 151–152
3-on-3 Trap, 120–121
360-Degree-fumble drill, 55
Through-a-blocker drill, 183–184
Through-a-man drill, 176–177
Through-a-man-to-the-ball drill, 222–
    223
Timing your plan, 20–21
Tip drill, 220–221
Tire drill, 242–243
Trap-vs-Stunts drill, 122–123
Trapping-the-board drill, 110–111
Trapping linemen, drills for, 107–125
    (see also "Pulling and trapping line-
    men . . .")
Trapping-the-Two-Man-Sled drill, 125
Triangle drill, 182–183
Twenty-catch drill, 218–219
Two-on-one drill, 140–141

U

Ups-and-downs drill, 250–251

V

Variety of drills essential for successful
    drill schedule, 24–25
Voit Power Arm Football, 241

W

Walk-through Tackling drill, 172–173
Warm-up drills, 29–55
    (see also "Agility and warm-up
    drills")

Wave drill, 52–53
Weight-training in off-season, 281–284
  reduction method, 281
West Point drill, 138–139
Whirl-out-vs-the-sled drill, 155–156
Whistle, using to end drill, 26
Whistle drill, 256–257
Wind-sprints, 276–277

Wrestling to knock off feet, 277–278
Wrestling to lift off feet, 278
Wrist bending, 278
Wrist-snap drill, 239–240

Z

Zone coverage drill, 224–225